# Wondering

*A book of writings*

David F. Palmer

A catalogue record for this book is available from the National Library of Australia


ISBN-13: 978-1-922343-97-0

Linellen Press
265 Boomerang Road
Oldbury, Western Australia
www.linellenpress.com.au

To Laura, Miranda, Sally and Julian,

Family is wealth beyond measure.

Cover Photograph by Laura K. Palmer

# Contents

# Author's Introduction

Dear Reader (or perhaps, Hapless Victim),

This collection of verse and prose has been accumulating in my 'never throw away a piece of paper' file for over three decades.  It is presented here because it seems to me that it is of no value to anyone sitting there, on the hard drive of my computer (or rather, computers – I have had many over the course of its accumulation) or tucked away in some file which will probably be disposed of upon my demise.

Even in this format, these writings may be nothing more than a desperate lunge at immortality by this pathetic soul. But you never know. Someone may get some pleasure or use out of them.

So here they are, in no particular order other than under a general collection in their respective types.

For those of you who are sensitive to gender issues, you will note that I have used the masculine form of the third person singular.  The reason for that is that I am a male, and that is the way that I normally think. No slight to female readers is intended.

Cheers.

David F. Palmer.
May, 2021.

# SAYINGS

# Creative Difference

The difference between an artist and an entrepreneur is that the artist doesn't care whether the customer likes the product or not.

The artist pleases himself.

# Boldly Go

Go boldly in the world.
And when someone asks of you: "Who are you to presume
to walk so tall?"
Answer: "I am a man and, for all my faults and failings, I do
the best I can."
And do.

# Speak Truth

Seek the Truth.  You will not find it
For reality will always be clouded
By your own ignorance, prejudice and lack of insight.
But try anyway.

Speak only what you believe to be true.
If you are wrong, someone who knows the truth will put
you right.
If you are right, what you know needs to be said
Or the world will forever live in ignorance.

## Regarding Wisdom

How does a man know if he is a fool or a wise man?
If he is a fool, people will tell him he is a fool.  But if he is a
wise man, people will still tell him he is a fool because they
won't understand what he is saying.

So, all you can do is to say what you think is true and do
what you think is right.

# A personal manifesto

Immerse yourself in beauty.  Wrap yourself in wonder.  Be brave. Aspire to excel. Crave harmony. Seek peace. Hope. Strive. Live. Love. Transcend.

# POEMS

# A Meaningful Life

When the eons of time have run their course, it will not matter a jot what we have accumulated in our lifetimes. For neither buildings, nor roads, nor monuments tall will stand witness to our efforts.
All will be swept away and not even the dust will remain.

But that we lived, and strove, and suffered, and triumphed in our own private worlds, will change the future of the Universe for all time.
For we each will have contributed to the great eternal outcome.

That we each existed, that we tried, that we added to the collective contribution of our race, no matter how modestly, is enough to justify our claim to eternal fame with equal right to anyone.

For the great deeds of conquerors and kings, of tycoons and potentates, of maestros and mystics, are nothing compared to the collective efforts of the common people.

Nor is the collective effort of the entire human race significant to the contribution of all the species that ever have, do now or ever will exist, on all of the planets of all of the star systems, to the collective consciousness of the Universe.

To make one's contribution and know that it counts is all that anyone can hope for. That is the meaning of Life.

# Cathedral

Glazed mosaics, pointed spires
Painted frescos, vaulted halls
Serfs and masters endless labour
Eons of devoted toil

Caverns sit in eerie silence
Faded tapestries hang slack
Twinkling candles flicker weakly
Lonely footsteps echo back

Monoliths in mist are shrouded
Haunted graveyards broken lay
Aging clerics shuffle slowly
Lonely widows hopeful pray

Is the dedication noted?
Does the prelate really care?
Is this house a welcome haven?
Is the spirit really there?

# Children

I think I am becoming to understand human beings.
When they are children, they act like children,
But, when they become adults,
They also act like children.


Blessed are the children
For they are innocent.
And in their ignorance
They show us up for what we really are.

# Dare

There is a spark in every human heart that lights a furnace of desire deep within the soul - a desire to be free - a desire to reach the heights of human experience.

This spark, when lit, gives birth to a flicker that grows to a flame and then to a fire-storm of passion that lifts the human condition to heights of undreamed glory.

To live; to love; to dream; to soar; to leave the Earth and all reality and simply go where your imagination takes you to a wondrous place of untold beauty bathed in glorious light with stirring music that drenches the senses in sheer delight - in ecstasy.

Every soul has this spark. Any thought can ignite it.  Any mind can feed the fire. Anyone can feel the joy.  But to do so you must take the time from of the bustle of life, to listen to your innermost self, to free your imagination and give your soul permission to fly. You must listen to the voice within that cries out for you to experience your humanity.

It is not a privilege reserved for the few. It belongs to you as your birthright.  It requires no money; no stimulant; no permission. All it needs is for you to have the courage to take what is rightfully yours.  Dare to be human. Dare to be free.  Let go of the bonds of guilt that bind you. Fly.

# Different

How big is "big"?  How far "a long way"?
What is normal?  How would you find out?
Who says it should be done like that?
It's fine to be wise when no longer in doubt.

Is that new?  Should we change?
Is it old because it was made yesterday?
It's obsolete!  Who says so?
It worked in the past; why not today?

Ignorance of the law is no excuse.
"Because I said so", that's all it takes.
If we know the difference 'tween right and wrong,
How come we all make so many mistakes?

What is insanity - being different in thought?
Am I insane 'cause I disagree?
And just being wrong, is that really so bad?
If no one gets hurt, why can't I think free?

How much is enough?  Do we really need more?
More junk? More stuff? Where can it be stored?
A soul filled with peace, or a belly too full?
More things, or more care?  Which would you choose?

What is love?  Is it really the best?
Eons of poets claim it to be ever thus.
If love conquers all, why do so many seem mean?
If love is so great, why does it hurt so much?

# Document

The paper sits on the table before me – the pen beside it. It is clean. Crisp. Its black ink lettering neat and tidy – the dotted lines, once vacant, now embroidered with a neat, meticulous scrawl. There it sits, beckoning me to add the final touch – the unique flourish that proclaims my acquiescence to its contents – my agreement (my surrender?).

I had hoped for more than this. I was confident I could get more.

But now, after months of trying, this is the sum of my promotion – this piece of paper – this final resolution. Take it or leave it. That's the choice.

Should I sign? Could I do better? I had thought so at the start. I was supremely confident. So much so that I had scornfully rejected an earlier deal – a better deal than this. But the market has deteriorated since then and will, I'm sure, deteriorate still further before this latest debacle has run its course.

But I could be wrong. I was wrong before. Oh, what torment hindsight.

There it sits. It goads me. "All this I will give you", it proclaims, "if you will only put your mark….just here". It taunts me. It mocks me.

What to do? What to do?

# Flatweed

Flatweed.  Flatweed?  Flatweed!
How dare you invade my turf?
Do you not know who I am?
I am man – Lord of the Earth.

Flatweed.  Flatweed!  Flatweed!!
I forbade you to enter my land.
Dare you ravage the harmony
I so carefully planned?

Flatweed, I banished you.
I chopped off your head.
I cut off your tap root and poisoned the soil.
Yet you still covet my garden bed.

Do you mock me, Flatweed?
Do you doubt my resolve?  Doubt me not,
Flatweed, do not challenge my claim
O'er this terrestrial plot?

Flatweed.  Why are you still here?
With your spreading leaves and your towering stem,
And your crowning orb of progeny.
Know you not that this is the realm of men?

Look, Flatweed, let's be fair.
You stay on your side; I'll stay on mine.
My needs are modest, half will suffice.
What say you, Flatweed? Can we compromise?

Up, Flatweed, Up. An alliance is best.
Now you have survived me and I dwell below,
Now this surface is yours and I slowly decay,
Feast on me, Flatweed.  Let me help you grow.

# Hero

What does a hero look like? We think we know. We see him (it is usually a "he" but not necessarily so – in fact, often not so) usually with a chest full of medals and a hat full of braid, uniformed, rank displayed (although not always of exulted status), deeds proclaimed in multi-coloured ribbons. And the hero is usually surrounded by fawning adulators proclaiming his fame. And pressing, ever pressing, to accompany him and bathe in his glow. Or so we think. So it seems.

But all that is a superfluity, garish show, the exercise of ego and awkwardness at our own ordinariness, our own ineptitude. And our self-conscious hero, feigning appreciation, politely acquiescing to the flattering attention, silently screams for release, for solitude, for time to quietly reminisce, to reflect, to escape, to forget.

Heroes know that it is not heroic to be a hero. It is terrifying. It is traumatic. It is everything other than what any rational, sensible human being would want to be. He knows. He alone knows. He craves to be nothing less than to be a hero – because to be a hero does not mean fame. It does not mean joy. It does not mean satisfaction. It means pain. It means suffering. It means trial.

Where do we find heroes? In the veterans' homes and the cenotaphs, to be sure – many there have strived and suffered – but not all bathe in glory. Some do – but few, precious few. But most heroes are not found there. Most dwell in more obscure places – where no one would think to look – where no one would even recognise them even if they saw them.

What does a hero look like? Is he filled with radiance, glowing with pride and magnanimity? Some are, but again, few – very few. Most heroes have a sullen look, sunken cheeks, sallow skin, bedraggled look, pathetic in countenance and stature, less in image than most ordinary mortals, not glowing, not imposing, not at all impressive.

So how do you know they are heroes? Look into their eyes. Look deep into their eyes. Look into their very souls. And there you will see a fire, a sparkle of defiance that refuses to surrender – beyond the grimace, beyond the wince, beyond the brave face and the false joke – there you will see, in tiny neon letters writ on pulsating background, a message scrawled and blazing brightly.

"I will not yield," it says. "I will not yield. I will not yield."

# Legacy

Here am I with wellness fading,
Product of the careless years.
Gone the zest of youthful vigour,
Gone the urge to lustful zeal,
Gone the spur of raw ambition,
Gone the dream of heights to scale.

Now with more genteel demeanour,
Tranquillity my favoured goal.
Comfort, kindness, passive transit,
The quiet search for a contented soul.

And whether peace will now prevail
Or cruel frustration overtake,
Mortality in the end will triumph
And my lifeless corpse disintegrate.

Were my efforts all in vain?
Have I well spent my time?
Surely.  For I have loved
And am succeeded
By progeny whole and fine.

# Lover's Prayer

L'amour.  Affairs of the heart.
Wild.  Intoxicating.  Desperate.
What madness overcomes us
When we feel the sting of Cupid's dart.

Blind.  Unheeding.  Unrepentant.
Speak to me not of My Love's failings.
I cannot see them.  Will not.  Dare not.
All I see is My Love – wonderful, addictive.

Oh the joy; the bliss; the ecstasy.
To be with My Love; to hold her; to feel her; to smell her;
To drink her in. Nothing else matters.
Nothing else can touch this marvellous feeling.

What pain!  What hurt!  What betrayal!
My Love has failed me.  My Love has deserted me.
My Love has cut me to the quick.
What have I done to deserve this?

Why does she spurn me?
Why does she gouge so ruthlessly at my tender soul?
She is flawed.  She is earthbound,
Not godlike, not divine, just human.

Run.  Hide.  Retreat.  Withdraw.
Protect yourself from this pain.
Never again!  Never again will I love.
It hurts too much.

But why me?
Why should I not have love?
Why not me too?
What have I done wrong?

Nothing – only expecting too much.
I am not Apollo.  I need no goddess.
Just a woman to love me
For myself – warts and all.

Let My Love have blemishes too.
Let me see them.
I leave perfection to the gods.
Next time, a human will be good enough for me.

Let My Love be flawed.
Let her be tainted with imperfections.
Let her see that I have faults too.
But let her also see that the good outweighs the bad.

Let her love me for all my faults – and let me love her the same way.

I will love again.

# Meld

Tonight I felt you. I really felt you.
I reached out in my mind and I touched you.
I really touched you.
I could feel the essence of your soul and I knew it was you.

How did I know that?
Because I know that you are just like me.
You are human – just like me. And you feel just like me.
Your soul, just like mine, yearns to connect with a soul-mate
Who understands how you feel.

I feel you. I feel your spirit. I feel the real you.
No. No, please, don't be embarrassed.
Don't shrink away.
Pause. Stay. Please, do not turn away.

I know you feel just as I feel.
You too yearn for understanding.
You too crave love.
You too seek joy.

Please, reach out to me.  Do not be afraid.
I will not harm you.
In your mind, hold out your hand.  Have no fear.
Gently, imagine holding out your hand.

That's right – calmly – slowly.
Now, touch my heart - tenderly.
Go on. I know you will not hurt me.
Go on. Yes. Like that. Just like that.

I can feel you. Can you feel me?
Do you feel my spirit? Do you feel my life force?
Can you feel it? I can feel you.
I can feel the very essence of you flowing into me.

Let go – meld into me. Let me meld into you.
I feel you. I feel your essence.
Merge with me – let us become one.
I can feel you flowing into me. I can feel us becoming one.

Oh.  Ohh. Oohh. I can feel it. I can feel it.
I can feel you mingling with me.
We are one. We are one.
I can feel it. We are one.

# Mobile

Deedle Um Dumb Dumb-dumb.
Deedle Um Dumb Dumb-dumb.
Deedle Um Dumb Dumb-dumb.
Deedle Um Duh….

"Hello"...
"Yes"…
"Er - I'm in a meeting right now"…
"Okay, but it'll have to be quick"…
"Yeh"….
"Yeh"….
"Okay. About five?"
"Okay",
"See ya."

"Sorry about that."

Deedle, deedle, deedle, deedle, dee.

# Morning Sigh

A wisp of mist danced across the morning air and paused briefly to await the next gentle gust before flitting onward to the next breathless pause.

It did not plan its journey nor did it intend to dally at any particular spot.

It just surrendered to the next gentle puff and moved off in response to its dictated dodging and weaving as the eddy met and passed each small bar to its way.

The wisp did this for its entire life, all forty-three minutes of earth time.

Then it disappeared as the morning sun's first rays beamed through the waking forest and bathed the natural ambience with their life-giving warmth.

It was a short life for the wisp but not without consequence.

A squirrel saw it and paused, dumbstruck, and marvelled at its beauty, and smiled inwardly as only squirrels can do, then scampered off towards its acorn store, enriched and enhanced by the romance of the sight.

# On Being Safe

Be at peace – nothing can harm you save your own fearful thoughts.

That body that you wear is not you.  It is merely the vehicle that you choose to travel in at this point in time. You are buried deep inside where nothing can reach you.

And, even if harm could pierce that puny flesh, it could not touch you - for you are elusive, formless, an apparition of pure consciousness that can move around, through or beyond anything physical.

And even when this fragile corpse can no longer carry you, you can quit its pathetic confines and move on to your destiny.

Be at peace. Only you can harm you.

# Oh God

Oh God! What form are thou, if thou be at all?
How would I know? How can I know?
Evangelists proclaim thee, devotees too.
But how can I know if they be true?

Great empires claim thee and threaten those who doubt.
Are numbers alone the measure of thy cert?
What proof do I have that you even exist?
Do I even need proof or will faith alone suffice?

Does life need meaning? Has the universe source?
Is there a reason for being, must there be a cause?
Is just being enough? Be thankful you're here.
Is more explanation needed?  Just enjoy the tour.

# On Doing Right

I do not know what more to say of truth,
Or justice, or beauty, but this:
None of us has wisdom so deep, nor ethics so pure,
That we know all of answers for sure.

So, all you and I, and other mortal souls,
Can do, is to do what we think is right,
Even when we're not sure
If it is good, or fair, or just, or true.

The thing that is the hardest
Is to venture forth bold
When you're not even sure
If you're on the right road.

The thing that is easiest is: do nothing at all
'cause then you don't have to make any call.
You are even excused your falt'ring response:
You can hide your fear behind feigned ignorance.

And sometimes doing nothing actually works.
Things sort themselves out, and that's sometimes good.
But it's not brave, or fair, or oft'n, even wise.
Doing nothing can lead to surrender to vice.

So, just do what you think is right and, if you are
Well raised, and decent, and honest, and kind,
Even if you are wrong, you will at least know
That you did your best. Who could ask of you more?

# On Hope and Despair

Hope is the light of the world.
All people need it.
Wretched are those who do not have it.

Despair is the eternal darkness.
No matter how high and mighty,
How rich or how powerful,
When Despair comes calling,
All are laid low.

No greater love has one human being for another
Than to bring them hope.
For no matter how wretched their condition,
The hope that things will get better
Is the reason for going on.

No greater ignominy can there be
Than to give hope to another falsely.
For to do so is a betrayal
Of the very reason of living.

Curse the charlatans. Hail the hope bringers.

# On Knowledge

Some things are
The way they are
Because if they weren't the way they are
They wouldn't be what they are.

Some things are known
Or, at least, believed to be.
Some things are unknown
But may be discovered.

Some things
By their very nature
Are unknowable.
They never will be known.

Get over it!

# On Law

We, the people, hold these truths to be
Self-evident, plain for all to see,
That we are all equal before the law,
Free born and slave (when I choose they be).

We fight for truth and liberty,
So you must rally to our righteous call,
And should you refuse, or attempt to flee,
Well, we deal with your kind up against a wall.

Our lord is love.  Dare you disagree?
You must believe, or show heresy.
Sacrifice is good in our noble cause.
Your reward will last for eternity.

You must yield.  My wrath is just.
Non-compliance means contempt, even more.
I need not seek that you acquiesce.
I have been empowered.  I am the law.

The God you doubt has bestowed on me,
Power over you - to inflict my will.
You cannot deny my legitimacy.
Might, alone, proclaims my authority.

# On the Fear of Death

What a wondrous thing this thing called life.
Just knowing that you are
And not knowing if you were before
Or will be again.
Being aware of yourself and hoping for more.

Why do we fear death?
When death must come to us all?
It is the one thing of which we can be absolutely sure.
Yet we don't know where, or when, or how we will die.

But, please God, not yet.

Why are we sad when we see others die?
Are we sad for them or sad for us?
If they are young, we feel sad
Because they did not get their full measure of life.
But what of the old, those who had a full life?
Why are we sad when they die?

What will it be like
When I am no more?
Will it be like when I am asleep?
And what is that like?
I'm not conscious then but it doesn't feel bad.

So why should I be afraid of dying?
I shouldn't be but I am.
I'm afraid because I don't know what it will be like.

I'm afraid of the unknown. Everybody is.

# Pachelbel in D

Dah dada dah dah. Dah dada dah dah.
Dah dah dee dah. Dah dah dee dah.
Dah dada dee dah. Dee dah. Dee dah.
Dah dada dee dah.  Dah dah dah.


I can hear the music, playing, play-ying.
I can hear the music: playing low.
I can hear the music: rising, falling.
I can hear the music calling me.

Dah dada dee dah.
Dah dada dee dah.
Dee dah.  Dee dah.
Dee dah dah.


Still the world keeps turning - turning, turning.
Still the world keeps turning.  I'm not there.
I am in a new world – new world, new world.
I am in new world somewhere else.

Dah, dah, dee dah.  Dah dah dee dah
Dee dah.  Dee dah.  Dah dah dah.
Somewhere in my new world.
Somewhere in my new world.
Somewhere in my new world filled with joy.


I am in my new world free from worry.
I am in my new world free from care.
Dah dada dee dah.  Dah dada dee dah

I am in my new world safe and free.

    I am in my new world free from fear.
    I am in my new world – won't come home.
    I am in my new world- new world, new world.
    I am in my new world…

# Prisoner

Deep within the soul of every person is a prisoner that yearns to be free. That prisoner is Good.

When each of us is born, Good is free. With the wide-eyed wonder of a child, it grows and develops, nurtured by the love and care of our parents and families. Aunts, uncles, grandparents, teachers, our formal institutions, in fact, the whole society, also aids its development by reinforcing the rules and values so lovingly bestowed upon us by those who raise us.

But as we grow older, we begin to realise that all is not as we were led to believe. Inconsistencies begin to emerge. Parents make excuses, drivers speed, taxpayers fudge, politicians lie. Our most cherished illusions begin to fade. The Tooth Fairy is not real – nor is Santa Claus. God seems more unreal and remote than ever.

As we move into adolescence and on into adulthood, a new awareness emerges. That awareness is Doubt. As Doubt grows, nurtured by life's experiences and the efficiency of modern communications, so too does its travelling companions: Suspicion, Cynicism, Hopelessness and Despair.

As the years pass, these parasites sap the energies of the soul. Our belief in Good fades along with its companions: Truth, Integrity, Hope and Joy. Doubt buries them and dares them to show themselves only upon pain of ridicule and retribution.

But Good is not dead. It is only stifled. And it lingers there deep within our soul, longing for the day when its jailer will turn the key and set it free.

Luckily, we know the jailer and we have the key. The jailer is us. The key is Courage.

# Rainy Day

Puh

         Puh

                      Puh

Puh           Puh

Puh  Puh             Puh  Puh  Puh Puh Puh

Puh Puh Puh Puh

Puh  Puuhh   Puppuh Puppuuhh Ssshhhhuusssshhhhh

Crack-a-crack               Sssssshhhhhuuuussshh

Bbbbbooooooooooommmmmm Baboom Boom Boom-

Boom Baboom Sssshhhuussshhhh Swish-swish Swish-

swish

Ssssssssssshhhhhhhhhhuuuuuuuuuuusssssssssssssshhhhhhhh

hhhh

Wwhhooohhh wooohh Crack-a-crack Woooh wooohhhh

Bbbboooommmm Babbooomm

Whooowoooo

Sssssssssshhhhhhhhiiiiiiiiiiiiisssssssssssssshhhhhhhhhhh

Shiisshhh  Sshhiisshh  Ciirrr   Iiiirrrr  Girgle  Girgle

Tttthhhhrrrrrr

Tunk Tunk Tunk Tunk          Tunk        Tunk

             Tunk                   Tunk

    Tunk

            Tunk

Tunk.

# Rebel

"I have a dream", he said, "all free at last.
Live up to the creed, it's self-evident".
"I am the light", he said, "go through me to Him".
"Trouble maker", they said, "better crucify him".

"From the barrel of gun – only way to win to power";
"No, sit down on the job, no one need get hurt".
"Burn that useless apparel, don't need that support,
We're not second class, we're the other half".

"It's unpatriotic", the President said,
"To change how things are.
Global trade means profits – more for all.
They need freedom and voting even if it means war".

255, I read yesterday, own half of all wealth.
Three billion or more, own one percent of the rest.
Have I read truth? Can that really be right?
Even if half true, surely that can't be just.

"Terrorists" they call them, all who resist,
The act clearly says so; talk of change is a crime.
"Part of His great plan", says the clergy.
God's will, my arse. It's obscenity.

# Religion of Humanity

Why is it beyond our wit
To understand that God is not
But that humanity is, the Earth is
And the Universe is also?

Why is it beyond our comprehension
To understand that there is no meaning to life
But that things are as they are
And that no further explanation is required?

Why does the Earth orbit the Sun
At the distance it does
And in the time that it takes
To make each orbit?

It does so because if it travelled faster, or further,
Or if it was more massive, or smaller,
Then its orbit would cease to be stable
And it would either crash into the Sun or fly off into Space
And the Earth, as we know it, would cease to be.

Why is life as it is, in all its wondrous forms?
Because that's the way it evolved.
If it had not done so,
Then it would not be life as we know it.

Who created the Universe? And when?
Who knows? Who cares? Does it really matter?
Why did anyone, or thing, have to have created it?
Why can it not always have been (in some form or other)?

Why can't we, each of us, realise
That we are here, now and in charge of our beliefs,
That each of us is unique and special,
And that we each have this wonderful gift called life?

Why can't we accept that the life that we have is all there is
That there is no "hereafter"?
That this brief period,
in which we are conscious of being alive,
Is the most precious experience any human being will ever
know.

And if we must love,
And it seems we must,
Why can't we love one another
And not some myth or deity?

Let us give to each other
Those things that will make the experience of life
As rich as it can possibly be.
Sustenance, respect, dignity, tolerance, care.

No more hate. No more war.
No more greed. No more want.
And no more Gods, temples, priests or dogma.
Only a Fraternity of Humanity dedicated to making this gift
of life
As rich as possible for everyone.

# Retirement

Waiting – nothing else to do but wait.
Sitting – could stand but why bother?
Wondering what else should I be doing
Now that I don't have to do anything?

Why is this such a problem?
This is what I have worked for.
All those years of toil and worry
Dreaming of the day that I could retire.

Now I have.
No more worries,
No more work,
No more "have to's.

But what on earth
Am I supposed to do now?

# Sea Eagle

High on a crag on a rock extending
Sits a pile of sticks in a circle tending
'Neath a blackened sky with the west wind howling
Lays a raptor's seed: his future pending.

Now but an orb frail and small
With needs aplenty from maternity
Will soon with mighty wings unfolding
Claim a majestic destiny.

Then from winged throne in an azure sky
Will he scan the ocean with piercing eye
And with meal located in the waters grey
With deadly talons seize his hapless prey.

Not through rage or anger will this fearful fate
On his victim visit, nor in lust or greed,
But on Nature's charge his motive base
To his strength sustain and his hunger feed

And when, in time, he becomes full grown
Will he woo and win a majestic dame
Then the royal pair from their sanctuary
Will make and grow their progeny

And 'ere too long from a rocky crag
On windswept isle with a towering height,
Will an anxious pair to heavens launch
A faltering chick on a cautious flight

But from natural breed will this youthful heir
To the heights ascend where no rival dare
And from there proclaim with piercing cry
His heritage: Lord of the Sky.

# Sinkiang

Nestled close to Asia's heart,
Lie ancient lands vastly spread.
Home of warriors eons distant
Proud traditions laced with dread.

Golden hordes of shepherds cantered,
Into history's annuls strode.
Laden trains of stately camels,
Tread a timeless silken road.

Views proclaim a rugged beauty
Cragged rocks in red and green.
Stony deserts endless stretching
Gouging floodplains torn between.

Towering mountains capped in ivory.
Glaciers in sunlight gleam.
Grasses bend to icy gusts.
Winter snows in blankets spread.

'Cross vast expanse of sparse terrain
Tented herdsmen tend their fold.
Patchwork fields of new sown planting
Weave green mosaics turning gold.

Ancient peoples' ageless lifestyles
Endure with strange ways overlain.
New arrivals seek a homeland
In this vast and peak-bound plain.

In the East the dragon rises
Claims a place in the global vein.
As the sun sets four-eyed eagles
Brood o'er a lost domain.

`Neath the crescent moon southward
Lonely voice wails heaven's fate.
In the heartland races mingle
Mix a brood potentially great.

At the crossroad wide tradition
Melds civilisation's latest breed.
'Neath the barren landscape nestles
Riches more than problems need.

Oh Sinkiang, your ancient glories
Hail the heritage you bare.
But a future dwarfing history
Is yours to claim if you but dare.

# Scientific Dilemma

On the television the other night, the physicists were talking about the Multiverse. It seems that we have gone beyond contemplating the Universe. It now seems that there are several dimensions of reality. And that they are all interconnected simultaneously.

I was having trouble before coming to terms with concepts like the Big Bang Theory, with Black Holes and Pulsars and all that stuff. Now it seems that the Universe is just one dimension. God knows what it all means. I doubt that anyone else does.

And that's another thing. Does God know? Does God even exist? The concept of God is just about as complex as the concept of the Multiverse.

I'm beginning to think that science is going down the same path as philosophy. No doubt the questions are interesting. No doubt they are profound. But can they ever be answered? Can they ever be proved? I doubt it.

More importantly, can these concepts ever be used in any practical way to elevate the condition of the Human Race? Sometimes I wonder.
How about you?

The scientists, of course, would say that gaining knowledge is valuable in itself. But is it? Is Knowledge valuable if you can't use it? And even if it is, what about speculation, conjecture, hypothesizing and theorizing? (Especially when theory can never be tested).

I wonder. I wonder if we are spending the world's resources wisely. With the vast sums we are ploughing into Science, would we not be better off just feeding the hungry, healing the sick and housing the poor?

Do we really get a good return from our investment in Science? And even if we do, do we all share in the benefits?

Oh, Heresy! Blasphemy! Shame!

# Sun God

Solar sphere, golden orb, shimmering disk,
Sinking slowly into the western sea.
Globe of light, brilliant, awesome,
Bathe me in your radiant glow.

Not for me the wonder of why men worship you.
Who could not be captivated by you?
Who could not be inspired by you?
I understand, Akhenaton, I understand.

Amun, Amun-Ra, Source of Energy,
Source of Life, Child of Creation,
Light my countenance; Warm my body;
Feed my sustenance; Power my world.

# The Hazard of Religion

Through the eons of time men have pondered the meaning of life. They wonder: "Why am I here? Where am I going? What is the point of it all?" To satisfy their craving for understanding men have turned to philosophy and religion for the answers.

Some, a very few, have dared to say: "I know the answer." These daring souls have laid out their answers in stories and in fables which other men have repeated and still others have written down. And these stories and fables have become the great religions of the world and billions have believed them.

But more than just believe them, the believers have become advocates for their particular faith, preaching it to others with passion and conviction, rejoicing when others have also become believers and despairing when they do not.

Rarely, very rarely, are they content to leave an unbeliever as an unbeliever. But often, they redouble their exhortation, intensify their passion, and press, very more firmly, their views on others.

And if the unbeliever resists their faith - even more, if he rejects it - then the pious believers turn to anger and their preaching turns to force. The pious believer, although professing to believe in love and brotherhood and tolerance, becomes a tyrant. He becomes an aggressor, a bully, and in his turning, he loses the essence of his faith. He becomes evil.

If you believe you have found the answers to the great questions of life then share them generously with all who seek your counsel. But do not offer your wisdom if it is not sought and do not press your beliefs on others if they do not welcome them. For that is the path of tyranny and the road to damnation. And the good that you seek to do will become a curse to you and to those you seek to enlighten.

# The Right to Rule

It is clearly plain for all to see
That our way of life is what should prevail
Our success alone proves it be so
No sane person could disagree.

So, we must cleanse this land of impure thought
To achieve our promised destiny.
Our cause is just, dare you not agree?
You must submit so you can be free.

We fight for good, truth and liberty.
All must rally to our righteous call,
And if you decline, or attempt to flee,
You will face your fate and your demise befall.

You must yield, our wrath is just.
Non-compliance is contempt of our cherished creed.
We need not seek that you agree.
Might alone dictates that we should succeed.

For I am law. I am right and true.
None can deny or challenge my rule,
I have the power to inflict my will
On everyone, even on you.

# True Wealth

Frantic.  Rushing everywhere.  All around, feverish activity.
Hustle.  Bustle.  Move it – NOW.
Why?  What is so urgent?
Why must everything be done in such haste?

Quiet.  Peace.  Serenity. Time.
How else can I hear the whispering of my soul?
How else can I discover what I really want
From this brief moment that we call Life?

Switch off. Close your ears. Close your eyes.
Listen only to your inner voice.
What is it that you really want?

Not this!  Not all this garish activity.
Not all this tacky junk.
Not all these gadgets.
Not all this noise.

Adequate resources for basic needs –
Air, water, food, shelter, companionship, belonging.
Beyond that, all else is superfluous, self-indulgent, greedy,
vain.

Seek truth, beauty, understanding and, above all, love –
Love for yourself, love for others.

That is true wealth.

# Tourist

Trains, planes and automobiles
Things with engines, things with wheels
Exotic foods, wondrous sights,
Walking trails, star-filled nights
Snoring late, drinking deep
Shunning work, vows to keep.

Is this reward for all my labours
Or just escape from annoying neighbours?
Travel now, travel often,
Much to see before a coffin.

But why so long before this break
Till decrepitude my strength will take?
Shouldn't I have lived 'ere this age
And strutted bold on history's stage?

No matter.  I am here now
Then someplace else 'ere the morrow.
And all that ignorance concealed
Will now, or soon, be revealed.

Ancient mysteries, secret rights,
Eerie customs, towering heights.
And I will surely understand
The vastness of the endless sand.

But wait, what is this that I see?
Houses, people, streets and roads
Rice fields, fish nets, boats with loads?
Children play, mothers dote,
Workers strain beneath the yoke.

Policemen sternly remonstrate,
Hecklers rile against the state,
Drivers curse, peddlers puff,
Promised gains yield little enough.

Are these sights all that queer?
Though sounds be strange to the ear,
Signs in gibberish, music weird,
Tastes exotic - illness feared?

Accents vary but motives clear
Mothers love their children dear
Fathers strive for future gain
Joy in living, dread of pain.

Unknown symbols rank displayed
Gestures subtle yet aim conveyed
Vibrant youth, some lived right through
Virtue urged and sin taboo.

Some folks trusted, others doubted,
Some admired, others spurned,
(Too) many poor but wealth here too.
Sounds familiar? How about you?

Is their world all that foreign?
Are these people so remote?
Do we not have much in common
With these strange exotic folk?

# Warrior

Arch right back and throw. And grunt when you do so that your spear will go a little further and strike your foe before he is in range to strike you. Because, if you don't, he may throw first and he may end your life before you have had a chance to prove your superiority.

And aim straight too. Don't throw wildly, in panic, in fear, even though you feel fearful and like running away. You will only have this one chance to pre-empt him. So don't miss.

Stay calm. Don't fret. Listen to your leader and follow his command. Trust in his judgment. He has been chosen because of his skill, his training, his experience and his coolness under stress. Trust his judgment as he trusts your skill and resolution.

Trust also your comrades beside you. They too have been well trained and are good stout fellows. You can rely on them as they rely on you. Together you will stand. Together you will win.

How trite it is to belittle marshal deeds. All the fawning peace mongers who sneer at your arts, your doctrine, your dedication and your honour, how crass that they think your efforts base, ignoble, brutal, dishonourable? How many of them have stood where you now stand, in a line like the one you now stand in? How many of them have faced the foe and dared him to advance knowing that he is totally focussed on your destruction and then ravishing all that you hold dear?

Heed not those who scorn you. They have no conception or understanding of what it is like to stand as you stand now. Only those who have stood thus understand. They do not mock you. They support you. They empathise with you even as they mouth a silent prayer of thanks that they do not have to stand with you this day. They have done their bit, in their turn, and they know what trial you face this day.

Listen to the veterans. And listen to your corporals, and sergeants, and captains, and colonels. They have stood their ground before. They know how to stand. They know how to fight. They know how to win. Believe in them. They are your best hope to survive and to prevail.

This calling, this profession, this persona you now wear, is an ancient craft, timeless, eternal. You are a warrior, the hope of your people, the champion of their safety and their freedom. Those who have worn this mantle before you have made it possible for everything that you love to endure. Now it is your turn.

Stand. Make strong your arm. Give your all – then find some more and give that too. You are honoured among men, especially all those warriors who have gone before you, over all the eons of time. Your strength, your courage, your unwavering steadfastness are your best shield and your strongest armour.

Now throw. Bellow a mighty cry. Then pause, wait for the command. Wait. Wait. Now! Now, brave warrior, into the fray.

# What Motive, Man?

Ruthless greed, soft compassion,
Wanton cruelty, selfless care,
Stupid impulse, brilliant vision,
Crass indulgence, generous flare.

What kind of beast is this race
That can be so fine yet be so base?
Be sometimes fair but sometimes mean
And oft' times swing in moods between?

Does he act on nature's spur
Or carefully choose what temper be?
Are his choices impulse-driven?
Or does he plan his strategy?

And how do my thoughts meet this trial?
Sometimes gentle, sometimes vile.
Sometimes caring, sometimes brute,
Mostly thoughtful, occasionally moot.

Would that I could understand
More myself and my fellow man
That I might harmony promote
In my inner self and with neighbouring folk.

# What's Important

The most important thing in the world is to like you. You don't have to like everything but, on the whole, you have to like yourself. There will almost certainly be things about yourself that you don't like, but mostly you can change these if you want to.

The second most important thing in the world is to love someone else. If you don't love someone else then it will be very hard for someone to love you. If nobody loves you, you will begin to doubt your own worth.

The third most important thing in the world is to like people generally. If you don't like people, you will only see the worst in them. But if you like people, not only will you see the good in them, you will also be able to forgive their shortcomings.

Health is important. It is hard to feel good about yourself, or about others, if you are ill or in pain. Look after your health as much as you are able.

Peace of mind is important. It is hard to be happy or healthy if you are always worried. Try not to worry. Try to be optimistic. Look to the future with hope.

Money is important, but only to the extent that you need it to sustain yourself. Needing money to impress others is a sign of your poverty not your wealth.

Likewise, needing fame, status or position is a sign of your lack of self-worth. The need to impress others shows your deficiency in self-esteem. It is good to enjoy the esteem of others. It is bad to need it.

Material possessions are the most unimportant things in the world. It is nice to have them, but if you need them, then you are very poor indeed.

# Whither hero?

In the Western sea 'neath the eagle's gaze
Lies languid giant on gluttonous spree.
Once proud champion of right and freedom
Now in hegemonic but arrogant pose.

In centuries past with words inspiring
Did this mighty warrior the world give hope.
With selfless forfeit did the hero herald
A shining vision of mankind's fate.

But the behemoth now doth weary look
And with fading interest more repose.
Though humanity's need has ne'er be greater
More self-absorbed the colossus grows.

Oh Columbia, where is your glow?
Have you gone the way of Britannia?
Where will we turn for hope and succour
If your courage has failed you and your goodness gone?

# Why?

If I had to write down for posterity
My greatest insight into the meaning of life
What could I say that would be of use
To all those who come after me?

The greatest question must surely be:
What is it really all about?
This thing we call life; why live at all?
For what great purpose are we all here?

Long have I pondered this great mystery
But wisdom seems to evade my quest
From decades toil and careful thought
Here is what I make of it all.

There is no reason, great or small
That tells the purpose of our lives at all
Miraculous though our passing be
Life has no purpose, there is no goal

It just comes forth and then declines
So, ponder not what your purpose be
Be glad you're here, enjoy the ride
Nothing more need be said

# Why Bother?

The Universe stretches
From the infinitely small
To the infinitely large
With no known bounds at either end.

Somewhere in the middle am I,
Trying to make sense of it all.
The only thing I really know
Is that I don't know.

Our intuition tells us
That there must be a reason for it all
But what that reason is
I don't know.

In any case, must there be a reason?
Why can't the Universe just be, without any reason?
Why can't I just be, without any reason?

And if there is no reason for it all – if it just is – if I just am,
Why am I bothering to try to achieve anything at all?
Why don't I just enjoy being, while I have the chance –
Before I cease to be.

# Woman

Oh woman why do you vex me so?
You told me twice –
You assume I heard.
Must you always have the last word?

What's that you say? I said what?
Well, I didn't mean it, even if I did.
Anyway, how was I supposed to know?
I failed mind reading. You should have said.

What is it, girl, that keeps me here?
You drive me crazy yet I love you dear.
All of your kind, not just you;
Mothers, daughters, lovers too.

Oh, womankind, all of your ilk,
From helpless babe to matriarch,
When did I fall with such hopeless yield
For these marvellous beings that share my world?

Primeval thoughts from the start of time
When female eyes first met mine?
When I lay helpless in her gentle arms
And she showered on me her maternal charms.

Or was on that fateful day
When a single glance took my breath away?
When I fell head-first 'to a chasm deep
And I couldn't think and I couldn't sleep.

Or ecstatic nights of unbridled lust,
The breathless strain of the final thrust
When my passion soared to climatic height -
La Petit Mort – the sweet delight.

Or later calm of serenity
When from slumber raised did a vision see
Of a moonlit breast rise and fall away
And the cool night breeze on our bodies play.

And thence from love and deep involve
With faltering steps and outstretched hands
Did our passionate issue my comfort seek
And with total trust in my arms did sleep.

Was it the cheeky laugh that won me too
When those tricks on me she did play?
Or twinge of loss on her joyful day
When I walked with a goddess and gave her away?

Now our mingled lives have reached full bloom
Can we claim the joys outweigh the tears?
Trials there were, though, in hindsight, few
And I do recall many happy years.

And still I see, passed the grey and grove,
With twinkling eye and defiant pose,
The playful imp, the proud princess,
Who won my heart all those years ago.

And is there something else I see?
A seductive glance, a subtle pose?
Is that a glowing ember I see?
Or is it just my memory?

# SONG LYRICS

# Jenny B.

**Verse 1:**

Jenny B was a singer, or at least she used to be
Strumming ballads slowly and crooning so softly
And in the smoke-filled bars of a faded yesterday
She brought peace to lonely souls with a longing lonely ear.

**Chorus:**

Oh Jenny, did you get what you came for?
Oh Jenny, did they hear your cry for more?
Oh Jenny, did it matter you came through?
Oh Jenny, would we be here without you?

**Verse 2:**

Jenny B was a lover, tender caring and sincere.
Holding hope and faithfulness to those she held most dear.
Standing back and waiting till her lover's taste was filled.
Patiently holding back while her tongue she held so still.

**Chorus:**

Oh Jenny, did you get what you came for?
Oh Jenny, did they hear your cry for more?
Oh Jenny, did it matter you came through?
Oh Jenny, would we be here without you?

**Verse 3:**

Jenny B was a mother, gave life to her child.
Protected and provided as the youngster's way was smoothed.
Loved and loyally sheltered her youthful protégé
As he strayed from innocence to a wild and wanton way.

**Chorus:**

Oh Jenny, did you get what you came for?
Oh Jenny, did they hear your cry for more?
Oh Jenny, did it matter you came through?
Oh Jenny, would we be here without you?

**Verse 4:**

Jenny B was a carer, the long lost hours endured.
Slopped and slaved in silent toil as suffering strangers called.
Washed and cleaned and lent a knowing smile
To the frail and helpless as they trudged their final mile.

**Chorus:**

Oh Jenny, did you get what you came for?
Oh Jenny, did they hear your cry for more?
Oh Jenny, did it matter you came through?
Oh Jenny, would we be here without you?

**Verse 5:**

Jenny B was dying, her last breath soon she'd take,
Waiting for the shining light to guide her to the gate.
Filthy ragged blanket wrapped around her slender frame
No one cared or understood or even knew her name.

**Chorus:**

Oh Jenny, did you get what you came for?
Oh Jenny, did they hear your cry for more?
Oh Jenny, did it matter you came through?
Oh Jenny, would we be here without you?

**Verse 6:**

Jenny B has gone now; did she ever live at all?
Nothing writ to signify her presence on the wall.
An angry man, a lustful beau, a long-forgotten sage.
People touched and then forgot as their fate too unfold'd.

**Chorus:**

Oh Jenny, did you get what you came for?
Oh Jenny, did they hear your cry for more?
Oh Jenny, did it matter you came through?
Oh Jenny, would we be here without you?

# The Old Blue Cloak

**Chorus:**

Lay me down once more for this final time
Now the twilight's fading and the tumult far
Drape my new hewn casket in that old blue cloak
With its five crossed stars gleaming
and its seven-pointed star.

**Verse 1:**

We did not venture forth because they made us go
Nor with belligerence nor lust for strife
Not for wealth nor glory nor a tyrant's call
But duty bound felt to our way of life.

**Chorus:**

Lay me down once more for this final time
Now the twilight's fading and the tumult far
Drape my new hewn casket in that old blue cloak
With its five crossed stars gleaming
and its seven-pointed star.

**Verse 2:**

Stirred by false conceit and vainglorious boast
From claimed reverence to proud legacy
With youthful zeal and a natural crave
For heroic quest and grateful history.

**Chorus:**

Lay me down once more for this final time
Now the twilight's fading and the tumult far
Drape my new hewn casket in that old blue cloak
With its five crossed stars gleaming
and its seven-pointed star.

**Verse 3:**

But 'ere too long it became quite clear
That with grotesque lie doth the valiant goad
Neither noble trial nor exciting game
Just pain, distress and tortuous road.

**Chorus:**

Lay me down once more for this final time
Now the twilight's fading and the tumult far
Drape my new hewn casket in that old blue cloak
With its five crossed stars gleaming
and its seven-pointed star.

**Verse 4:**

And once enlighten to the awful truth
We did not fight on to be rich or free
Nor devotion to a leader or the greater cause
I fought for my comrades and they fought for me.

**Chorus:**

Lay me down once more for this final time
Now the twilight's fading and the tumult far
Drape my new hewn casket in that old blue cloak
With its five crossed stars gleaming
and its seven-pointed star.

**Verse 5:**

And through rain and heat and blinding storm
So many stumbled, so many fell
And with trembling hand and a tearful eye
We bore homeward from that manmade hell

**Chorus:**

Lay me down once more for this final time
Now the twilight's fading and the tumult far
Drape my new hewn casket in that old blue cloak
With its five crossed stars gleaming

and its seven-pointed star.

**Verse 6:**

Now my time has come to join that band
Of comrades gone and oft ignored
I wonder why we still resort to war.
Why not settle difference through quiet accord?

**Chorus:**

Lay me down once more for this final time
Now the twilight's fading and the tumult far
Drape my new hewn casket in that old blue cloak
With its five crossed stars gleaming
and its seven-pointed star.

# ESSAYS

# Author's Note re Essays

The first item in this section is the final synthesis of a series of five essays on the nature of religion which was first published on the website of the *Centre for Research on Globalization*, in December 2008, and which is still available at

http://www.globalresearch.ca/index.php?context=va&aid=11485.

This is followed by a few thoughts on the seeking of wisdom and then an item on nature of leadership within democratic political systems.

# A Thesis on the Nature of Religion

No supernatural being or beings exists that is or are responsible for the creation of the Universe or for its continuing functioning. (This is the fundamental axiom of an atheist's viewpoint but it is a necessary starting point if the writer is going to be honest with anyone who might read this thesis.)

There are Laws of Nature that do determine the functioning of the physical universe but those laws are inanimate, unconscious and not purposeful. But they do have universal effect.

Desire for the perpetuation of life is a genetic characteristic of all living things. Any species that does not possess this characteristic will not survive. This is also known the survival instinct.

Love is a universal phenomenon. It is necessary for survival inasmuch as many species, including humans, are unable to survive without the support of others of their kind. Being loved is essential to survival. Loving another is essential to ensure reciprocal love in return. Loving and being loved are therefore essential to human survival. The survival of someone who loves you is therefore essential to your own survival.

Belief in a supernatural being or beings is very widespread amongst the human race, almost universal.

Belief in a supernatural being or beings is a psychological construct, a pure creation of the human mind. (This is my fundamental thesis and it flows naturally from the initial atheistic axiom).

Human beings have created the psychological construct of religion essentially as a defence mechanism to enable them to cope with the realization of their own mortality. (This is a basic hypothesis of this theory).

The essence of this coping mechanism is the hope that death is not the end of an individual human's existence but merely the end of this particular phase of existence. Death is a readily apparent phenomenon. The hope of life after death is therefore an extension of the survival instinct.

Concern over the welfare of loved ones is also a universal phenomenon. The loss of a loved one is a traumatic and threatening psychological experience for any who experience it. It is therefore universally sensible and attractive to believe that a departed loved one is not gone but merely residing in another place. This is a psychological defence mechanism to assuage one's sense of loss. As such it is a natural part of the grieving process.

No human being knows how to make the hoped-for transition from this phase of existence to the next. None who have died and are presumed to have made the transition have returned to tell those still living what the afterlife is like. Nor have they been able to explain to potential travellers how to make the journey. Since no human knows how to do it, it is necessary to create a non-human facilitator who can effect or aid that transition.

Since no human being has the power to facilitate such a transition it is necessary to endow the created facilitator with supernatural powers to enable that entity to successfully undertake the task.

The replacement of a lost lover by a surrogate is essential

for continued psychological, if not physical, health. Where no human surrogate can be found, it is necessary to create a non-human lover. A mythical being can fulfil this psychological need if no living surrogate can be found. This provides a psychological defence against the loss, but it cannot provide material support. Other mechanisms are required to provide material support to the survivor.

Each human civilisation has evolved and is evolving within a unique geographic and temporal space. As a result, each civilisation creates, endows and articulates the nature and attributes of its conception of the supernatural facilitator in a context that is understandable to its contemporary population.

The universality of these concepts is accomplished through the mechanism of a deeply felt and widely accepted psychological phenomenon. It is the collective psyche of huge numbers of people, whole civilisations. (This is another central plank in this theory). I call this phenomenon 'Universal Understanding'.

Universal Understanding embodies the hope of, if not the belief in, the possibility of an immortal life. It also embodies the hope of, if not the belief in, the existence of a mechanism for achieving it.

Since the conception of a supernatural entity requires that such an entity must have supernatural powers to be able to perform its primary function, the facilitation of the hope-for transition to the next phase of existence, it is sensible, reasonable and convenient to assume that such an entity is also able to deliver other extraordinary benefits besides the phase-transition. These supplemental benefits include: rescuing individuals from danger; protecting loved ones; delivering favourable environmental conditions; bestowing rewards for meritorious acts; and delivering a feeling of being loved to those who feel unloved.

Universal Understanding incorporates the shared visions, myths, concepts and ideas of all groups that have been in contact and have interacted with one another. It accepts, incorporates and instils these concepts into each civilization's own cultural and temporal context because they appeal to the deep yearning of all human beings for the fulfilment of their basic psychological needs. These needs include: a sense of being special, belongingness, self-worth, security and enlightenment.

The appeal of these concepts is so pervasive because it promises the fulfilment of basic psychological needs that are common to all human beings.

The understanding of and belief in these concepts is transmitted between separate and distinctive human groups – within, and between, tribes, peoples, races, cultures, nations and civilisations – through the various communications media that exist, and have existed, over time and space. These media have allowed ideas and artefacts to be exchanged between diverse groups. They include such media as language, art, symbols, writing, mythology, history and memory. They are included both in contemporary exchanges and the transmission of meaning over time. (This is another central plank in this theory).

Meaning is transmitted through the physical senses, not through any spiritual or telepathic media. Much of this communication is subconscious, including such mechanisms as body language, ambience and subliminal cues. These phenomena are well known to psychologists and are widely used by politicians, clergy, advertising agencies and other communications practitioners.

Religions differ in their conceptions of deities, of life after death and of the mechanisms of the phase-transition because of: the divergent physical demands of the respective habitats of their devotees; the degree of contact of those devotees with the devotees of other civilizations; and with the unique historical journeys of their respective peoples.

Each religious tradition has evolved a distinctive set of rituals that are administered and policed by a special fraternity that is sanctioned and authorised to do so by its society. This is the priestly class.

The political structure of each human group is afforded enhanced legitimacy by securing religious approval from its priestly class for the empowerment of its political elite. The crowning of kings by bishops and popes, the swearing-in of political leaders by religious leaders, the establishment of basic laws and regulations such as the Ten Commandments and the Qur'an, are examples of this authorisation.

Hence, the religious and political elite of each tradition has a vested interest in reinforcing belief in its particular conception of the supernatural being and in the enforcing of its particular rituals to the exclusion of other competing ideologies. Acknowledging the legitimacy of other traditions actually undermines the legitimacy of the ruling elite and calls its authority into question.

Religious intolerance actually promotes, encourages and reinforces the legitimacy of the privileged position of the political and religious hierarchy of a particular elite group over its subjects. Religious tolerance actually presents those subjects with an alternative to their current ruling regime.

The principal control mechanism of the priestly class is the threat of ex-communication of the laity from the deity. This severance denies the laity both access to contemporary benefits emanating from the deity and to the transmission services of the deity after death. That is, the priestly class controls access to contemporary supernatural benefits and also access to immortality.

The principal control mechanism of the political class is the threat of and actual application of physical violence against the laity for non-compliance with its dictates.

Religion denies the laity the right of appeal to the deity to redress this violence because the deity, via the approval of the priestly class, has already sanctioned and approved the elite's use of violence.

All law is based on the threat of violence by the political hierarchy for non-compliance of its dictates. Where this threat is ignored, the actual use of violence is authorised by the law. Religion provides the ultimate authorisation for the application of the law by the political elite as anointed by the priestly class on behalf of the deity.

Divine authorisation for the empowerment of the elite is the preferred mechanism for social control because it is presumed by the laity, and actually claimed by the priestly class, that the deity operates from a higher level of knowledge, wisdom and understanding, coupled with supernatural powers, than that of ordinary human beings, individually and collectively. The deity is also presumed and claimed to be incorruptible. These are both highly desirable characteristics for most people. Who would not wish for, admire, even love, a benevolent overlord with such characteristics?

The central problem with religion, however, is that neither the priestly class nor the political elite has been able to demonstrate or prove the actual existence of a deity or deities. Neither have they been able to prove that any entity, divine or otherwise, has such characteristics. Moreover, the promised benefits of the deity are not necessarily bestowed by the deity on the laity when requested.

If religion is essentially based on wishful thinking, then it cannot be relied upon as the basis for either law or morality. Therefore, mankind will need to develop other mechanisms upon which to base legal and moral principles. Those principles will need to be universally agreed if corruption and manipulation by unscrupulous and self-serving individuals is to be avoided or remedied.

Since the promise of an afterlife cannot be fulfilled, human endeavour must be focused on: the greatest level of fulfilment for all people currently living and the creation of a world environment that will ensure the greatest level of fulfilment of the lives of future generations.

To ensure the survival of the human species, God cannot be the ultimate authority to which mankind is answerable. Humanity collectively must be.

# Knowledge is the key to survival

What is it about human nature that yearns to have someone who knows the answers to those questions that we do not know ourselves? Is it just natural curiosity, or is it something more fundamental to our nature? Or is it something that is inherent to our own particular culture at this point in human history? Or is it universal to all peoples at all times?

It is not difficult to appreciate that some level of knowledge is necessary for human survival, especially a detailed knowledge of the risks and opportunities of one's own immediate environment. Failure to appreciate the local risks could result in one's early demise. Lack of appreciation of local opportunities could also be detrimental inasmuch as local benefits may go unidentified. This could be particularly detrimental in times of stress, even fatal.

So, knowledge of one's own immediate environment would appear to be vital to one's own wellbeing and to those we rely on or care for.

But is it really necessary to acquire more knowledge once immediate physiological needs have been met and do not appear to be in jeopardy?

The vagaries of weather and other natural phenomena might suggest that it is prudent to ensure future survival, to build up a certain level of reserves in such vital resources such as water, food, shelter and general security as a buffer against unexpected contingencies. But how much reserve is prudent given that the accumulation of reserves is costly in terms of time and resources: days, weeks, months, a full season; what, how much is enough?

Some human cultures, particularly those living in areas of abundance, do not seem to see the need to create extensive reserves. Their experience up to a point has suggested that the needed resources will always be available. So, they see no need to create reserves and choose, instead, to just live day to day.

In other cultures, the abundance of resources is so scarce that the creation of reserves is not possible. All available time and effort is required just to survive on a daily basis. In such societies, not only are resources scarce but there is no time available to pursue knowledge beyond that which is required for immediate survival. For a similar reason, there is no time to pursue new knowledge for its own sake. Hence there is little technological progress.

The quest for knowledge, however, is not confined to the accumulation of technological capability. Knowledge is also sought due to natural curiosity, driven by the quest just to know the unknown. Why? What good is knowledge if it can't be used to enhance the wellbeing of human beings? Is it something that we do because it is biologically built into our DNA? If we did not have the instinct to seek new knowledge, would we have progressed to our current state of wellbeing? Probably not.

Solutions to problems are sometimes found through chance, but more often than not, we find solutions to problems because we see analogies between the situation at hand to other situations in which we know the causes and effects. The transposition between the two analogous situations is often not linear or logical. The link often occurs purely because of human imagination. So, knowing something, even if not immediately relevant, does not mean that it might not become useful at some future point in time.

Could that be the key to the success of humans as a species, a fortuitous quirk of our particular makeup? Maybe. Perhaps it is one of a suite of fortuitous traits that evolved within us. We do seem to be somewhat unique in that regard.

The quest for new knowledge seems to be a prized pursuit amongst technologically advanced cultures. Perhaps it is the reason for their success. Those cultures which do not prize the pursuit of knowledge do not seem to enhance the individual wellbeing of their constituents, in material terms, at least. In those cultures, tradition is more highly prized than progress. And in competitive environments, it is the technologically advanced cultures that seem to prevail in the long run. Perhaps this also contributes to the survival of technologically advanced cultures, anyway, if not the less sophisticated ones.

Yet even technologically advanced cultures, advanced for their age, that is, ultimately tend to meet their demise. So technological advancement alone is not the key to survival; there would seem to be a need for other sustaining features besides mere knowledge itself. The maintenance of other necessities is also required.

To ensure their survival, knowledge that they are at risk is also vital. Ignorance of risk is fatal. Failure to mitigate those risks is also culturally fatal. But knowledge of risk, where none was previously perceived, is, in and of itself, new knowledge. So simply assuming that things will stay the same is also ultimately fatal. Survival itself requires the constant monitoring of all vital resources required for survival. Ignorance of change, in all its forms, is fatal.

In summary, then, cultures that do not pursue the

acquisition of new knowledge will likely be those that are least likely to make the connections between apparently unrelated phenomena, will not perceive analogies and will not cope well with change. So, they will not adapt. They will not be the survivors. The traditionalists will be those who will be more likely to become extinct.

# Looking for Leadership

I have come to the belief that the world is moved forward more by the geeks, weirdoes and social misfits that toil away in the workshops, back sheds, computer nooks, studios and similar creative haunts than by the glad-handing baby-kissers and rear-anatomy-defenders that inhabit the legislature and the bureaucracy.

My experience with government, and with politicians, in particular, is that you can spend enormous amounts of time and effort trying to win their support only to yield very modest results.

If they do actually help you, it is usually by referring you to someone else. And the people to whom you are referred will then, in turn, usually refer you elsewhere, and so on — an endless round-robin of duck-shoving.

If by some miracle, they actually amend legislation or even allocate a small portion of next year's budget (much, much less than you asked for) to assist your cause, their initiative usually ends up being of greater benefit to the rich and powerful, who don't really need the help, rather than you, the struggling champion who sought their help in the first place.

I think our belief that "the government should do something" stems from a fundamental misunderstanding of the nature of democracy — the belief that we elect our political leaders to lead. I would argue that, by definition, in a system where the "leader" is dependent upon the support of the majority, a politician cannot lead. "Leadership" means "going before" and encouraging others "to follow". In such a system, the "leader" cannot lead until the majority is ready and willing to follow. Wise politicians know that.

As for bureaucrats, it is patently absurd to expect a person who has spent decades deftly and cautiously tip-toeing through the bureaucratic minefield – subtly, but ruthlessly, vanquishing rival aspirants for high office – to put all of his or her gains at risk just to support the whims of a total stranger for the benefit of other total strangers.

No, my friends, it is not politicians or bureaucrats, or even academics or clerics, that change the world. It is those devil-may-care, crash-through or crash-and-burn, irrepressible, undeniable souls – those who just keep persisting when all rationality and logic tells them that they must fail but press on regardless – it is they who change the world.

Back the dreamers with stars in their eyes and passion in their hearts. It is they who will further your cause. The politicians and bureaucrats will fall into line soon enough – when the outcome becomes obvious.

# RESEARCH REPORTS

# Author's Note re 911 Research Activities

We now move on to what I regard as the serious section of this narrative, my quest to understand the true nature of the extraordinary events that took place in New York City on the 11th of September, 2001 (commonly known as 911).

In July 2005, I purchased a book from Amazon.com entitled *Crossing the Rubicon* by Michael C. Rupert[1]. In it, Rupert, a former Los Angeles Police Department narcotics investigator, expressed the view that if he had been in charge of the investigation into the mass murders that took place in New York on that day, he believes that he has sufficient evidence to lay criminal charges against the senior members of the Bush Administration for the crime of mass murder. To my mind, it is an astonishing book. But having read it, I said to myself: "Boy, that's an amazing story." Then I quietly filed it on the bookshelf in my study and proceeded to reach for the next book on my reading list.

A few years later, I came across an academic paper entitled: *Active Thermitic Material Discovered in Dust from the 9/11 World Trade Centre Catastrophe*[2]. I noted that one of the authors of the paper, Frank Legge, had recorded a business address in Subiaco, a suburb in the Western Australian capital city of Perth. So, I looked up Dr Legge in the local trade directory and called him up on the telephone. I said to

---

[1] (New Society Publishers, Grabriola Island, BC, Canada, 2004)

[2] Harrit, Niels H., Farrer, Jeffrey, Jones, Steven E., Ryan, Kevin R., Legge, Frank M., Farnsworth, Daniel, Roberts, Greg, Gourley, James R. and Larsen, Bradley R., *Active Thermitic Material Discovered in Dust from the 9/11 World Trade Centre Catastrophe*, The Open Chemical Physics Journal, 2009, 2, 7-31.

Frank: "Look, I'm not a technical person so please tell me if I'm reading your paper correctly: are you telling me that the Twin Towers of the World Trade Center were brought down by a controlled demolition?"

Frank simply said: "Yes."

There are some moments in life that change your world forever. That "yes" from Frank Legge, coupled with the insights provided by Mike Rupert a few years earlier, changed mine.

The following year, the lead author of the abovementioned research paper, Professor Niels Harrit, came to Australia and gave a single public lecture in Sydney. Having been forewarned of the event, I flew over to Sydney from Perth specifically to attend that lecture. At the half-time interval of the event, I went up the Prof. Harrit and introduced myself. The following day, I also met Dr Legge, who had also flown over from Perth to participate in the same event, in person.

On the flight back from Sydney the next day following, I commenced drafting what later become my own paper entitled: *911 Research Report – an Australian Perspective*. I have since published that report as an Appendix to my novel *Amerissance: American Renaissance*. Since that paper (and its later addendum) has already been published, I have not included it in this volume.

The two reports that follow document some of my later attempts to enlighten the Australian Government and the Australian people about 911. The first, entitled *Updated Summary of my 911 Research Activities*, reiterates much of what the previously above-mentioned report and its addendum said, plus a later paper entitled *Why I believe that the Official Narrative on 911 is suspect*, which also essentially reiterated what the aforementioned report said, together with additional insights inserted in some points. It also updates my research activities up to the end of September 2016.

The second paper included below, entitled *My attempts to speak Truth to Power in Australia with respect to the 911 Event* reports my most recent attempts to enlighten the Australian Government on this issue in 2019 and 2020.

# Updated Summary of my 911 Research Activities.

By David F. Palmer*

In my *"911 Research Report – An Australian Perspective"* of 2010 and my *"Why I believe that the Official Narrative on 911 is suspect"* paper of 2012, I essentially expressed the following conclusions about the events that took place in New York City and in Washington D.C. on 11th September 2001 (known colloquially as "the 911 terrorist attacks" or more simply as "911" or "9/11". I personally prefer the term "the 911 event" for reasons that will hopefully become clear below:

    a. The official version of the events of 911 by the United States Government (USG), and particularly its key agents in the matter, the Fire and Emergency Management Authority (FEMA), the National Institute for Standards and Technology (NIST) and the 911 Commission, are, at least, inadequate, if not a complete whitewash. They are simply incredible – that is, not believable.

    b. An alternative hypothesis that the collapse of World Trade Center buildings number one, two and seven (WTC1), (WTC 2) and (WTC 7) was due to a controlled demolition is at least as credible as the official explanation for their collapse which proposes the "Progressive Column Failure (PCF)" hypothesis as the main cause – in fact more so in the light of the evidence now available in the public domain, some of which is cited below. So, the "Controlled Demolition" hypothesis should be more formally and more thoroughly investigated as a serious scientific hypothesis by academic and professional researchers.

c. The best that can currently be said about the 911 event is that it is an unsolved mass murder. The main reason that it has not yet been solved is, I believe, because the USG refuses to conduct a proper criminal investigation into the crime.

My reasons for arriving that these conclusions are set out below.

In the almost twelve years that I have been researching the 911 event, I have come to regard the following facts as being "reasonably certain" (or, if you like, in legal terms, "proven beyond reasonable doubt"):

1. The official 911 narrative as proclaimed by the USG is false because:

   a. There is no plausible scientific reason why the aircraft impacts between the 92$^{nd}$ to 98th and 78$^{th}$ to 84$^{th}$ floors of the North Tower and South Tower respectively of the World Trade Center should have caused both towers to collapse <u>all the way to the ground</u>. Peer reviewed scientific papers by Szuladzinski et al and by Korol et al demonstrate that the "PCF mode" hypothesis, which forms an integral part of the official USG

911 narrative, is implausible.[3] It should be noted that NIST's investigations of the collapse of WTC1 and WTC2, the twin towers, did not address the reasons for the collapse of the floors below the point of impact of the aircraft which struck the buildings. It only examined the sequence of events that occurred between the time of impact of the aircraft and the "initiation of collapse". The actual PCF hypothesis was first proposed by Bazant et al[4] in a paper written just a few days after 911 which NIST only refers to in a paragraph in its final report (NIST NCSTAR 1-6 at page 323). Of this, NIST says: "The study performed by Northwestern University (Bazant 2002) was a simplified approximate analysis of the overall collapse…[It] did not address impact damage, fire dynamics, or structural response of the towers. Rather a generalized condition was

---

[3] See Szuladzinski, G, Szamboti, A, and Johns, R, *Some Misunderstandings Related to WTC Collapse Analysis*, International Journal of Protective Structures, Volume 4, Number 2, 2013, pp117-126 for a persuasive discussion in which they cite three "fatal mistakes" in the Bazant et al paper (see note 4 below) which supports the official version of why the North Tower collapsed. See also Korol, R.M., Sivakumaran K.S. and Greening, F.R., *Collapse Time Analysis of Multi-Story Structural Steel Buildings*, The Open Civil Engineering Journal, 2011, 5, 25-35 and Korol, R.M. and Sivakumaran K.S., *Reassessing the Plastic Hinge Model for Energy Dissipation of Axially Loaded Columns*, Journal of Structures, Volume 2014 (2014), Article ID 795257, 7 pages for a report on their physical experiments on the buckling of metal columns subjected to axial loading and a discussion of the more generalized engineering principals involved.

[4] Bazant, Z. and Zhou, Y., "Why did the World Trade Center collapse?-simple analysis," *Journal of Engineering Mechanics*, vol. 128, no. 1, pp. 2–6, 2002, Addendum to *Journal of Engineering Mechanics*, vol. 128, no. 3, pp. 369–370, 2002.

assumed". But NIST then went on to say that it agrees with the assessment[5]. So, the NIST report <u>does not</u> provide a full explanation of why the twin towers collapsed all the way to the ground – it merely accepts Bazant's explanation of why it did. And the two abovementioned peer-reviewed scientific papers persuasively contest Bazant's conclusions.

b. There is no plausible reason why WTC7 should have collapsed as a result of the office fires allegedly started by falling debris from WTC1 (the North Tower). No steel-framed high-rise building had ever collapsed completely due to fire before 911 and none has done so since. At the *Justice in Focus 911* conference in New York City on 10th September 2016,[6] Professor Leroy Hulsey from the University of Alaska, Fairbanks, presented his preliminary findings into what <u>did not</u> cause WTC7 to collapse. He did so with the accompaniment of a power-point presentation which ended with a slide asking: "Did WTC7 collapse from fire?" The slide then immediately answered this question with a simple word: "No". This is in direct contradiction of the NIST report of November 2008 entitled "Final Report on the Collapse of World Trade Center Building 7"[7] the abstract of

<hr>

[5] Available at <u>http://fire.nist.gov/bfrlpubs/build05/PDF/b05040.pdf</u>
Extracted 21st December 2016.
[6] I attended this conference as an audience participant.
[7] Available at
<u>http://ws680.nist.gov/publication/get_pdf.cfm?pub_id=861610.</u>

which summaries NIST's findings with the words: "This report describes how the fires caused by the debris from the collapse of WTC1 (the north tower) led to the collapse of WTC7". So NIST says that WTC7 "probably" [see point c. below] collapsed due to fire. Hulsey definitively says: "No, it didn't".

c.  Video footage, from several different angles, of the collapse of WTC7 shows that this building collapsed symmetrically so all of the support structures right around the building must have failed at approximately the same time and not in the sequential manner suggested in the PCF explanation provided by NIST. NIST's abovementioned report says that it "performed computer simulations of the behaviour of WTC7 on September 11, 2001; and combined the knowledge gained into a <u>probable</u> collapse sequence". NIST's graphical presentations of its simulations shows significant deformations of the building structure[8] which are totally absent in the video records of the actual collapse. Moreover, NIST has refused to provide a large portion of its modelling data that was used to perform its simulations on the grounds that to do so "might jeopardize public safety". NIST's explanation as to why and how this building

---

[8] See Figure 3 in the brochure entitled "Fifteen Years Later: On the Physics of High Rise Building Collapses" by Steven Jones, Robert Korol, Anthony Szamboti and Ted Walter available at http://www.europhysicsnews.org/articles/epn/pdf/2016/04/epn2016474 p21.pdf. I met Anthony Szamboti at the Justice in Focus 911 conference referred to in this paper.

collapsed is therefore incomplete, suspect and hence implausible.

d.  Over 150 eye witnesses to the events of 911 in New York City reported hearing "explosions" or "bombs" exploding before and during the collapse of all three buildings. Video footage also shows on-site journalists reporting on these events flinching and ducking at the sound of explosions clearly heard in the background of their broadcast locations even before the buildings started to fall. Video footage of New York firefighters clearly shows them explaining the sight and sound of sequential explosions as they watched the buildings falling. Explosions were clearly involved in the collapse of all three buildings yet NIST says it did not look for any signs of explosives being used because it says that there was no evidence to suggest that they were. Clearly, NIST ignored large amounts of evidence pertaining to this event because that evidence contradicted its <u>preconceived</u> conclusions about what caused the collapse.[9]

e.  A scientific paper by Harrit, Jones et al reported finding traces of unreacted nano-thermite residues in four dust samples collected from

---

[9] Professor Graeme MacQueen from the University of Toronto has reviewed over 11,000 pages of eye-witness testimony from those present in New York City on 911 and reports the abovementioned findings. He is featured in the DVD "911 in the Academic Community", a documentary by Canadian film maker Adnan Zuberi, which exhorts academics around the world to conduct more rigorous research into the 911 event particularly addressing the question "What actually happened?" I have exchanged e-mails on several occasions with both Professor MacQueen and Mr Zuberi and have satisfied myself as to their credentials, professionalism and sincerity and I subsequently met Professor McQueen on 8th September 2016 at a film festival in Oakland, California.

Lower Manhattan in the hours and days after 911. This paper provides scientific proof that explosives were involved in 911. I have met personally with Professor Harrit and another co-author, Australian chemist Dr Frank Legge, to verify their credentials and the veracity of their paper[10]. Their paper provides valid scientific proof that explosives were used in the destruction of the WTC buildings.

f. Seismic survey data from the Lamont-Doherty Earth Observatory of Columbia University, in Palisades, N.Y, a seismic observatory some thirty four miles away from the World Trade Centre, shows that ground disturbances originating from the 911 events in New York, and which were initially explained as depicting aircraft impacts and falling debris, have now been reinterpreted by Rousseau so as to demonstrate that the nature of the waves, their velocities, frequencies, and magnitudes invalidate these officially adopted explanations.[11]. This reinterpretation constitutes further scientific evidence which contradicts the official story about 911.

g. If explosives were involved in the destruction of WTC1, WTC2 and WTC7 then someone must have had access to those three buildings prior to

---

[10] Harrit, Niels H., Farrer, Jeffrey, Jones, Steven E., Ryan, Kevin R., Legge, Frank M., Farnsworth, Daniel, Roberts, Greg, Gourley, James R. and Larsen, Bradley R., *Active Thematic Material Discovered in Dust from the 9/11 World Trade Centre Catastrophe*, The Open Chemical Physics Journal, 2009, 2, 7-31.

[11] Source: http://www.journalof911studies.com/resources/RousseauVol34November2012.pdf. Extracted: 2nd September, 2014.

911 to place those explosive charges. Significant maintenance and upgrade activity is known to have been undertaken in the Twin Towers in the months prior to 911 with the full authority of the owner of the Twin Towers, the Port Authority of New York and New Jersey, and head lessee of those two buildings, and owner of WTC7, New York businessman Larry Silverstein.[12]

h. It is unreasonable to assume that Al Qaida or any other Islamic terrorist organization could have gained access to all three buildings to place demolition charges without being detected, particularly in WTC7, which contained the New York offices of the CIA, the Department of Defense and the Securities and Exchange Commission. Therefore, whoever placed such charges (if the Controlled Demolition hypothesis can be credibly sustained – and some commentators referred to above and below believe that it already has been) must have had assistance from someone with unfettered and unquestioned access to all three buildings – someone sufficiently credible to all who saw them so as not to challenge them or query what they were doing.

i. None of the airliners involved in 911 was intercepted after they were reported as being hijacked even though under normal procedures

<hr>

[12] Details of these renovation and maintenance activities can be found in Ryan, Kevin R., "Demolition access to the World Trade Center towers", a four part expose commencing at http://911review.com/articles/ryan/demolition_access_DonPaul.html. Extracted: 27th July, 2010.

there would have been ample time for them to do so. Air Force jets were scrambled dozens of times earlier that year to intercept troubled or suspected aircraft. Why did they fail to do so on 11ᵗʰ September 2001? Maybe because:

   i. Intercept procedures were changed a few months before that day.

   ii. Multiple exercises were taking place on 911 – many more than usual.

   iii. An extraordinary number of available US Air Force interceptors had been redeployed to northern and western locations, away from the northeast sector, to participate in these exercises.

   iv. Radar imagery on 911 was confused by the injection of dummy signals into live radar monitors as part of those exercises.

   v. There was a disruption of the military chain of command on 911 with an inexperienced officer being placed in command whilst his superior absented himself from his post. The latter was never disciplined for this breach of duty. Rather, he was promoted.

None of these unusual Air Force manoeuvres could have been arranged by Islamic terrorists. Much of the detail of these manoeuvres is reported in Michael C. Ruppert's book "Crossing the Rubicon"[13]

---

[13] *Op cit*, New Society Publishers, Gabriola Island, 2004.

j.  A scientific paper by Professor Amparo Sacristan Carrasco, an acknowledged expert on image analysis, reports that the apparent cylindrical shapes shown in photographs of the aircraft that struck the South Tower (WTC2) were real physical objects and not aberrations of the light.  Boeing 767-300 commercial aircraft have no such attachments. This leads to the obvious conclusion that the aircraft that struck the South Tower was NOT a commercial airliner. This evidence also constitutes scientific evidence that the official story is wrong. I have met personally with Professor Carrasco to confirm her credentials and the veracity of her paper[14]. She also signed a copy of her paper in my presence as evidence of its authenticity and I now have a copy of that signed document in my possession. In addition, whilst at the *Justice in Focus 911* conference in New York on 11th September, 2016, Mr William Jacoby, secretary of the newly launched 911 Truth Action Project told me that he knew of an eye witness to the impact of this aircraft into the South Tower who reports that the aircraft that she saw hit the building was not a commercial airliner.  She said that the aircraft that she saw was all grey, with no identifying markings on it and had no windows along its side. As a result, I believe that Professor Carrasco's evidence provides

---

[14] Source: http://www.amics21.com/911/report.html. Extracted 10th January 2011.

independent corroborating evidence to this eye-witness's testimony.

k. The co-chairs of the 911 Commission complained that the resources they were provided with to carry out their inquiry were inadequate to do the job and that they were given too little time. They expressed the view that they had been "set up to fail". They also complained that their efforts had been hampered by members of the Bush Administration, the CIA and the Department of Defense.

These are the main arguments that form the basis of my abovementioned conclusions about the 911 event, but there are many more, dozens in fact, of anomalies, inconsistencies, irregularities and misinterpretations that could be added to the above list which, even if they do not rate as "reasonable certainties" as described above, could justifiably be listed under the headings of "unanswered questions" or "unsatisfactory answers". American writer David Ray Griffin has listed over one hundred such additional facts which could be so classified. His paper "The 9/11 Commission Report: A 571-Page Lie" summarizes his findings.[15] The 9/11 Consensus Panel lists over 40 points which its review panel considers to be "best evidence" that the official narrative on 911 cannot

---

[15] Source:
http://www.911truth.org/article.php?story=20050523112738404.
Extracted: 10th August 2010.

be true[16].

2. As a result of the above, I believe that we cannot rely upon the current U.S. Government propounded narrative on 911 as being a credible explanation of what happened on that day. A fresh inquiry is clearly needed.
3. The contents of the press release covering the *Justice in Focus 911* conference noted above are worth considering here[17]. Some of its more insightful comments include:

"We had the unprecedented opportunity to present before this esteemed panel of legal professionals the forensic evidence that three WTC skyscrapers, WTC 1 and 2 – and WTC 7, not hit by any plane – all featured the key signatures of controlled demolition," said Architects & Engineers for 9/11 Truth founder and president Richard Gage, AIA.

"As Arthur Conan Doyle famously said, 'Once you've eliminated the impossible, whatever remains, however improbable, must be the truth'," said Lawyers Committee for 9/11 Inquiry Vice President Mick Harrison, "and <u>the evidentiary presentations established these forensic facts beyond any reasonable doubt</u>." [My underlining – Note that it is a group of eminent lawyers that is expressing this opinion.]

"And how did the official authorities deal with all of this [physical and eyewitness] evidence of controlled demolitions?" asked Professor Emeritus Graeme

---

<sup>16</sup> See http://www.consensus911.org/the-911-consensus-points/ for a list of these points.
<sup>17</sup> The full two-day program and access to the archived videos are at www.911justiceinfocus.org and www.noliesradio.org.

MacQueen, a member of the 9/11 Consensus Panel and co-editor of the *Journal of 9/11 Studies*. "The answer is simple. They didn't. … All my studies of the eyewitness testimonies conclude that explosions [independent of plane impacts and resulting fires] brought down these buildings."

"The September 11th attacks are one of those high crimes that can cause the very foundations of the law to tremble," said renowned public interest attorney Daniel Sheehan.

The upshot of this New York conference is that its final event was the calling of an impromptu board meeting of the Lawyers' Committee for 9/11 Inquiry on the same stage where Abraham Lincoln delivered his famous Cooper Union Address in which the board members, there being an adequate quorum present, passed a resolution to proceed with compiling an application to a US Federal court of appropriate jurisdiction and also the courts of appropriate jurisdiction in the states of New York and New Jersey to convene a Grand Jury in each or any of these jurisdictions to conduct a new investigation into the events of 911. The committee is firmly of the opinion, both legally and historically, that those inquiries that have been conducted since the tragic 911 event have been woefully inadequate and that no proper criminal investigation has ever been carried out into what is undoubtedly an unsolved mass murder. The committee has also concluded, based on the evidence now available, that the current official US Government sanctioned conspiracy theory of the events of 911 cannot possibly be true and that the evidence of its falsehood is overwhelming.

5. It should be noted that it was not just Americans who died on 911. Ten Australian citizens were amongst the victims of this crime. So, this is not just an American problem. It is our problem too.

6. Greens candidate for the 2016 U.S. Presidential Election, Jill Stein, on 9th September, 2016, called for a new investigation into 911 saying:

> "Led by the families of those who died on 9/11, the American people wanted – and deserved – a comprehensive and independent inquiry into the attacks. The Bush administration initially said an inquiry was unnecessary, claiming that the perpetrators had been identified and their methods and motives were clear.
>
> It is well known that the 9/11 Commission produced a report containing so many omissions and distortions that *Harper's Magazine* described it as "whitewash as public service" – a document that "defrauds the nation." The co-chairs of the 9/11 Commission wrote a book just two years after the final commission report, saying, "We were set up to fail." The 9/11 Commission was not given enough money, time, or access to relevant classified information" and "The families and friends of those who were murdered on 9/11 deserve justice… They also deserve to know the truth."[18]

---

[18] See http://www.theblaze.com/stories/2016/09/10/jill-stein-calls-for-new-investigation-to-find-the-truth-about-911/

7.  The main reason that I am so concerned about the way that our response to 911 has unfolded is because of the danger that it poses to the core values that we profess to believe in. We profess to believe in personal freedom, democratic government, rule of law and human rights. How can we continue to maintain and pursue these core values if we allow nearly three thousand people to be murdered in broad daylight with the whole world watching but then ignore large swathes of evidence pertinent to the event and avoid conducting a proper criminal investigation into the crime? If we continue to do so then we are allowing the true perpetrators of this crime to get away with murder. And if we allow that to happen how can any of us have any confidence that we are safe and protected by the political, judicial, legal and military institutions that we have established and maintain to secure our lives, liberty, property and the pursuit of a happy and fulfilling life for ourselves and our loved ones? All of the core values noted above are at risk if we do not deliver justice to those who have suffered as a result of this crime.

*David F. Palmer is a retired management consultant living in Western Australia. Prior to that, he practised as a Chartered Accountant, during which period he was, among other things, a Registered Company Auditor. In both professions, he conducted numerous investigations into anomalous situations.

Of my previous writings on the 911 issue, which are noted in the introduction above, the first, *911 Research Report...*, was forwarded to the key political parties in

Australia in November 2010 and directly to the Prime Minister's office in May of the following year with a later addendum thereto. It was also forwarded to the Australian Federal Police in September 2011.

My second-mentioned paper, *Why I Believe…*, was forwarded to similar addressees in 2012.

No official response has been received from any of the addressees save for an automated e-mail response from the office of my local member of parliament acknowledging receipt of them.

## My attempts to speak Truth to Power in Australia with respect to the 911 Event

Over the past decade, I have attempted to bring to the attention of the Australian Government, and the Australian people generally, the fact that there is substantial and persuasive evidence now available in the public domain that proves beyond reasonable doubt that the official United States Government (USG)'s account of what happened in New York City and Washington D.C. on 11th September 2001(commonly known as 911) cannot possibly be true.

In the main, my attempts to do so have been unsuccessful.

Laid out below are examples of my most recent attempts to bring to the attention of Australia's political leaders facts, not theories, that are now readily available to anyone who cares to look, that 911 was "an inside job". These facts are detailed in two lawsuits that are currently before the American courts, together with a newly published report from the University of Alaska Fairbanks, which proves that World Trade Center building number 7 (WTC7) was brought down by a controlled demolition. Since it takes weeks, if not months, to rig a building for controlled demolition, this report alone proves that 911 must have been pre-planned by people with unfettered access to that building.

The response of the Australian Government to my advices has been to, firstly, ignore them, and then, subsequently, to censor my reports to them on the subject.

The particular vehicle that I used to convey my latest set

of advices to the Australian Government was the requirements of the recently passed Foreign Influence Transparency Scheme [FITS] Act 2018, which, by coincidence, required that an organization for which I was then the Australian spokesperson, Truth Outreach Inc. doing business as 911 Truth Action Project (911TAP), met the definition of a "foreign political organization" as defined by that act. The act required me to report all of my outreach activities in my capacity as spokesperson for 911TAP to the Australian Government in the prescribed manner.

The emails cited below provide evidence of the attempt by the Australian Government to censor my communications to them on this matter. Although somewhat repetitious, they do show the diversity of my attempts to convey this information to both the media and the government.

**Text of an Email sent to Australian Politicians on 4th September 2019 #1**

"Greetings all,

I bring to your attention that the draft final report of the study into the collapse of WTC7, the third building to collapse in New York City on 911, by Professor Leroy Hulsey of the University of Alaska Fairbanks is available for download here: https://www.ae911truth.org/wtc7.

The study entailed the construction of a detail computer simulation constructed from the construction drawings of the building for the entire building and subjected to vigorous testing and verification. On page 111 of the report, Professor Hulsey concludes that:

> "The simultaneous failure of all core columns over 8 stories followed 1.3 seconds later by the simultaneous failure of all exterior columns over 8 stories produces almost exactly the behavior observed in videos of the collapse. The collapse could have started at various floors starting at Floor 16 and below and produced the same behavior.
>
> It is our conclusion that the collapse of WTC 7 was a global failure involving the near simultaneous failure of all columns in the building and not a progressive collapse involving the sequential failure of columns throughout the building."

The US$300,000 four-year study was commissioned by Architects and Engineers for 911 Truth (AE911Truth), a section 501(3) non-profit organization which has 3,131 architects and engineers who have called for a new investigation into the collapse of all three buildings on 911, the Twin Towers of the World Trade Center (WTC1 & 2) and the 47-story WTC7, which was not hit by an aeroplane, but which collapsed straight down into its own footprint eight hours after the collapse of the Twin Towers.

The report directly contradicts the report on the

collapse of WTC7 by the National Institute of Standards and Technology (NIST) which was the official US Government agency tasked with explaining why the building fell down. NIST acknowledges that their explanation that office fires alone caused the collapse would have been the first time in history that a steel framed high-rise building collapsed solely due to fire. NIST proposed the progressive collapse hypothesis as the basis of its conclusions which Hulsey's study specifically disproves.

AE911Truth has expressed the view that the only way that they are aware of that such a collapse can occur is by the use of demolition charges. According to AE911Truth, no other plausible explanation is possible.

Since it takes months to prepare a building for demolition, for WTC7 to have collapsed just hours after the initial aircraft impacts, then the collapse must have been planned and prepared long before 911 occurred, by people who had unfettered access to the building in the weeks and months prior to 911.

In other words, Professor Hulsey's report PROVES that 911 was an 'INSIDE JOB'. This is NOT a 'crazy conspiracy theory'. This is now PROVEN SCIENTIFIC FACT.

Sincerely.

David F. Palmer."

#1 The specific politicians addressed were: Senator Reynolds, Senator Siewert, Senator Steele-John, Senator Payne, Andrew Wilkie, Christian Porter and Madeiline King.

Reports by persons who are required to register with the Foreign Influence Transparency Scheme (FITS) are called "registrations".

## Text of a FITS Registration by me on 9th September 2019

"Commenced distribution of a flyer that reports the release of a report on 3rd September 2019 by Professor Leroy Hulsey from the University of Alaska Fairbanks which proves that World Trade Center Building number 7 was demolished by explosives on 11th September 2001. WTC7, which was directly across the street from the North Tower of the World Trade Center, was not hit by an airplane but it collapsed straight down into its own footprint eight hours after the twin towers collapsed. Professor Hulsey's report PROVES 911 was an INSIDE JOB."

A copy of this flyer under the title *WTC7 Simulation Disproves NIST Report* is reproduced below.

## Text of an e-mail from me to the National Press Club on 13th September 2019

Ladies and Gentlemen,

This morning I sent the following e-mail to four Australian senators and three House Representative and several other private individuals:

"Greetings all,

Please be advised that on 11th September 2019 the President of the Lawyers Committee for 911 Inquiry (LCfor911Inquiry) held a press conference at the National Press Club in Washington DC in which he advised that the Lawyers Committee had lodged with the abovementioned court [the District Court for the Southern District of New York] a petition requesting the court to order the US Attorney for the Southern District of New York to disclose whether or not he had empanelled a Grand Jury to receive and consider the evidence it had submitted in its petitions of 10th April 2018 and 30th July 2018 (a copy of the latter of which is available here:

https://www.lawyerscommitteefor9-11inquiry.org/lc-doj-first-amended-grand-jury-petition/) and , if not, to order the US Attorney to empanel such a Grand Jury.  On 7th November 2018 the US Attorney advised that he would comply with the law in respect of this petition but when asked in July 2019 if he had actually done so the US Attorney declined to say so due to the secrecy requirements of Grand Jury processes.

LCfor911Inquiry President, Attorney David Meiswinkle's address to the press conference may be viewed here:  https://www.lawyerscommitteefor9-11inquiry.org/. In his press conference address, Mr Meiswinkle expressed the legal opinion of the lawyers committee that the evidence of controlled demolition of the Twin Towers of the World Trade Center (WTC1 and 2) and of the Salomon Brother Building (WTC7) on 11th September 2001 by the use of explosives was 'dispositive', a legal term which he explained meant 'beyond doubt'.

Sincerely,

David F. Palmer

This material is communicated by David Frank Palmer on behalf of Truth Outreach Inc. AKA 911 Truth Action Project. This disclosure is made under the Foreign Influence Transparency Scheme Act 2018."

In addition, I have recently distributed the attached flyer [now entitled *Scientific Report Proves 911 was an inside job* and with the 911TAP logo and FITS disclosure added] to several university campuses in Perth. It reports the finding of a four-year US$300,000 study by Professor Leroy Hulsey of the University of Alaska Fairbanks which concludes that for World Trade Center building number 7, WTC7, to have collapsed in the manner in which multiple video recordings show it collapsing could only have occurred if ALL of the support columns holding up the building failed at the same time over eight floors of the building (or, within 1.3 seconds of each other according to Hulsey's report). The non-profit organization Architects and Engineers for 911 Truth Inc., AE911Truth, which has collected the signatures of over 3,000 architects and engineers calling for a new investigation in 911, states categorically that the only way that they are aware of that this could happen is by the use of demolition charges.

The evidence that the official US Government's explanation as to what happened in New York City on the 11th September 2001 cannot possibly be true is overwhelming. Or, to use the phraseology of the above quoted American Attorney, David Meiswinkle, the evidence that the three steel-framed high-rise buildings that collapsed in New York on that day were demolished by the use of explosives is 'dispositive', or 'beyond doubt'.

Isn't it about time that Australian journalists grew a backbone and started reporting the truth of this event instead of perpetually regurgitating the total and utter bovine manure that the United States Government, and its lackey, the Australian Government, have been peddling these past eighteen years?

Sincerely,

David F. Palmer

This material is communicated by David Frank Palmer on behalf of Truth Outreach Inc. AKA 911 Truth Action Project. This disclosure is made under the Foreign Influence Transparency Scheme Act 2018.

**Text of an e-mail from me sent to the National Press Club on 14th September 2019**

"Ladies and Gentlemen,

Following my email below ['below' refers to the email of 13th September as cited above here], can I direct your attention to the 1.38 minute video clip available at this site (shown by Alaska TV station KTVA):

https://www.ktva.com/story/41015153/fire-did-not-cause-world-trade-center-building-7-collapse-uaf-study-suggests

Could you not at least report this?

Cheers.

David Palmer.

This material is communicated by David Frank Palmer on behalf of Truth Outreach Inc. AKA 911 Truth Action Project. This disclosure is made under the Foreign Influence Transparency Scheme Act 2018."

**Text of an e-mail from me sent to Media Watch on 14<sup>th</sup> September 2019 #2**

I sent an e-mail to the National Press Club this morning which says: "can I direct your attention to the 1.38 minute video clip available at this site (shown by Alaska TV station KTVA): https://www.ktva.com/story/41015153/fire-did-not-cause-world-trade-center-building-7-collapse-uaf-study-suggests. Could you not at least report this?" In a previous e-mail to them [I] said, inter alia: "Attorney David Meiswinkle's address to the press conference [at NPC Washington] may be viewed here: https://www.lawyerscommitteefor9-11inquiry.org/" which reports the same event.

Could you please incorporate this information in your next Media Watch broadcast? Come back to me if you need any further information or a full copy of the two e-mails I sent to them earlier.

This material is communicated by David Frank Palmer on behalf of Truth Outreach Inc. AKA 911 Truth Action Project. This disclosure is made under the Foreign Influence Transparency Scheme Act 2018."

#2 This message was sent via Media Watch's on-line messaging facility rather than via my traditional Outlook e-mail app.

**Text of an email <u>from FITS</u> to me of 30<sup>th</sup> September 2019**

"Dear Mr Palmer

Thank you for your email advising that you are ceasing activity with your foreign principal. We are grateful for your consistent diligence in ensuring your compliance with the scheme.

We are now in the process of finalising all your details so that your activities can be ceased on the register. To that end, we intend to make the following changes:

1. For your communications activity of 13-14 September, we intend to retain the following: "Email sent to Media Watch on 14th September 2019 reporting a broadcast of station KTVA Alaska available here: <u>https://www.ktva.com/story/41015153/fire-did-not-cause-world-trade-center-building-7-collapse-uaf-study-suggests</u> and emails to the National Press Club in Canberra reporting the same KTVA broadcast and also an address by the President of the Lawyers Committee for 911 Inquiry to the National Press Club in Washington DC on 11th September 2019 which is available here: <u>https://www.lawyerscommitteefor9-11inquiry.org/</u>. Both e-mails requested that these events be reported in Australian media." **<u>We will delete the rest of the description</u>** [My bolding and underlining here].

2. Your communications activity for 7 September and 9 September appear to refer to the distribution of the same flyer. Please confirm whether this is the case. If so, we intend to delete the activity for 9 September.

3. If they are not the same, **we intend to alter your description** of your communications activity from 9-29 September to read: "Commenced distribution of a flyer that reports the release of a report on 3rd September 2019 by Professor Leroy Hulsey from the University of Alaska Fairbanks arguing that World Trade Center Building number 7 was demolished by explosives on 11th September 2001." [My bolding and underlining here].

4. On your Parliamentary Lobbying activity of 7 September, we intend to correct a minor spelling error (Marice Payne to Marise Payne).

5. **We intend to alter your Parliamentary Lobbying activity** of 4 September to read: 'E-mail to four Western Australian senators, to the members for Brand and Dennison advising: "I bring to your attention that the draft final report of the study into the collapse of WTC7, the third building to collapse in New York city on 911, by Professor Leroy Hulsey of the University of Alaska Fairbanks which is available for

download here:
https://www.ae911truth.org/wtc7." **We
intend to delete the remainder of the
description**. [My bolding and underlining
here].

The alteration of these descriptions is to ensure that they are
an <u>appropriate length</u> and are not <u>overly politicised [my
underlining here]</u>. The FITS register is for the purpose
stating the activities engaged in rather than existing as a
platform to spread a message or persuade an audience. We
take the same approach with all registrants, regardless of
their political stance. Similarly, we allow businesses to
provide a factual description of their activities but do not
allow them to sell or promote products on the register.

Please advise your understanding of this and provide the
requested information by COB Wednesday 2 October in
order for us to correctly cease your registration.

Thank you once again for your ongoing diligence and
engagement with us.

Yours faithfully

**Isla Moyse**
| T:+61 2 6141 3222| E: transparency@ag.gov.au"


In terms of <u>appropriate length</u>, it should be noted that the
longest of the above registrations was 463 words whereas
FITS allowed 850 words for registrants to report their
activities on their registration site. As for being <u>overly
politicised</u>, one might wonder why else a citizen would

lobby a politician if not with respect to a matter of government policy or to change existing legislation.

I replied to this email on the same day as follows:

**Text of my email to FITS on 30th September 2019 in reply**

"Thank you for your advices below [above as presented here]. I can confirm that my flyer of 7th September is indeed the same flyer as used on 9th September.

As for point 3. below [above as presented here], I would point out that if you were to publish that version it would, in fact, be false and misleading. Professor Hulsey, in his report, does not say that World Trade Center Building number 7 was demolished by explosives. He has, in fact, persistently declined to say that. What Professor Hulsey says is that the only way he could get his model of building 7 to collapse in the manner in which it was observed, as shown in numerous videos of the collapse, was to remove all of the core columns on floors 5 to 13 simultaneously and then 1.3 seconds later to remove all of the peripheral columns for the same eight floors simultaneous.

When asked at the Q&A session immediately following his presentation: "How could that happen in real life?" Professor Hulsey replied: "I'm not going to go there". It was the sponsoring organisation, Architects and Engineers for 911Truth Inc., that says that the only way that they know such a collapse

132

could happen in real life is by the use of explosives. Their opinion is supported by the 3,200 architects and engineers who have signed their petition calling for a new investigation into 911. Thus, it is their interpretation of Hulsey's report that states that the building was demolished by the use of explosive.

The interpretation that Hulsey's report proves that 911 was an inside job is my interpretation. But I do not think that that is a fanciful conclusion on my part nor in the minds of my former foreign principal. I think that any reasonable person would draw that conclusion. And I think that any twelve good and true citizens sitting on a trial jury would come to the same conclusion also.

I have since reported back to Truth Outreach Inc. AKA 911 Truth Action Project my decision to terminate my arrangements with them. I had asked the president of that organisation for a clear instruction for me to 'cease and desist from representing myself as being an official representative of, or a spokesman for, Truth Outreach Inc. AKA 911 Truth Action Project, if that is what he wanted me to do. He has emailed me this morning instructing me to 'desist'. His instruction seems quite clear to me and confirms my previous understanding of his position. I can supply you with copies of this correspondence if you require.

However, I have subsequently amended the headline of that 9th September flyer to: "Scientific Report proves that 911 was an Inside Job" which is the conclusion that I have drawn at the bottom of the flyer. I have also now removed the 911TAP logo from the flyer and also removed the FITS disclosure from the bottom of the document. This is the version that I will use going forward although I will await your final confirmation that I have no further obligations under the FITS act before undertaking any further outreach activities which cites 911TAP in any way. The other two organisations which I have cited from time to time – namely, Architects and Engineers for 911Truth Inc. and Lawyers Committee for 911 Inquiry Inc. – do not, in my opinion, meet the definition of a 'foreign political organisation' and, in any case, I have no direct relationship with either of them.

I appreciate your patience and courtesy throughout this exchange. For what it's worth, I did not set out to use FITS as a broadcasting medium. It [was] only when I realised that you offered the facility to post extended messages via this medium that I decided to use it for that. Quite frankly, I was surprised just how much latitude you were affording me. I didn't know if it was an oversight on your part or whether you were affording me this opportunity because I was saying things that I knew that Australian government could not say. My later posts were designed to test just how far you were prepared to let me go. I'm not displeased with the compromise you have settled for.

As far as I know, nothing I have told you was false or misleading but I can see why you now need to be guarded. The American government would go ballistic if they thought you were publishing the truth about 911 on an Australian government website. That would make them very angry. And if they were to slap an arms embargo on Australia in retaliation, that would seriously affect Australia's national security, it would render the Australian Defence Force inoperative within weeks.

So, in terms of your instruction: "Please advise your understanding of this", that is my understanding of your policy. I'm not saying you're wrong, your remit is, after all, protecting Australia from foreign influence. It's just a shame that the parliament legislated to exclude the American government in its scope of the threats that we need to be wary of. But your job is to administer the laws that parliament passes so I do understand your position.

So why do I persist with this quest? Because 911 was a crime, a mass murder, in which ten Australian citizens lost their lives. Furthermore, we lost 41 Australian service personnel in Afghanistan, fighting a war that we should never have been involved in because that whole conflagration was based on a lie. There has never been a proper criminal investigation into this crime. That is what my former foreign principal and its associated organisations are trying to achieve.

The other reason I have been active on FITS is because it affords me a direct line of communication to ASIO and the AFP instead of the circular methods that I was using previously. It enables me to assure them that I personally do not pose a threat to anyone, **unless the truth itself be a threat**, but that at the same time it enables me to keep them abreast of a number of initiatives taking place in the USA which, if successful, and I'm quite confident that they ultimately will be, will have a significant impact upon US foreign policy and, in consequence, on Australian foreign policy [My bolding here].

The other thing that you might like to know is that, despite now formally instructing me to 'desist' speaking for 911TAP here in Australia, the president of that organisation has reiterated his request for me to continue in my role as unpaid consultant to 911TAP and he has invited me to participate in their upcoming executive meetings and their upcoming board meeting. I'm still considering whether to accept those invitations.

Please advise if you require anything further from me at this time.

Sincerely,

David Frank Palmer"

A record of my registrations with the Foreign Influence Transparency Scheme (FITS) can be viewed on the FITS Public Register at the following website: <u>Transparency Register - Transparency Register (ag.gov.au)</u>. Just click on the linked marked 'Registrants' and go to page 3 to my name 'David Palmer', click on the 'View Details' link and read the seventeen (17) registrations I made under this scheme. You will note that the entries altered by FITS read as they indicated they would amend them in their email of 30th September 2019 cited above. FITS have also altered my reports to them (my 'registrations') in my private account so as to record their amended versions of what my reports say not the full text of my communications as I actually reported them and as I have cited them above.

A copy of the flyer I posted on numerous public notice boards in the July to September 2019 period reporting the progress of the law suits cited above that were being undertaken in the USA at that time are also included below although those printed versions were reproduced in two-column A4-size one-page format.

The purpose of this report is to place on the published record evidence of the fact that the Australian Government, and the Australian media, have been informed of the truth about 911 but have persistently refused to acknowledge that truth or that they have been made aware of it. You can see their response, or lack thereof, above. The response of the media has been to ignore me. The response of the Australian Government has been to censor my writing so that the essence of my reports is obscured.

Compiled by David Frank Palmer at Shoalwater W.A. on 19th May 2021.

# WTC7 Simulation Disproves NIST Report

#3

A draft final report of the study into the collapse of WTC7, the third building to collapse in New York City on 911, by Professor Leroy Hulsey of the University of Alaska Fairbanks, was released on 3rd September 2019. A copy of the report is available for download here: https://www.ae911truth.org/wtc7.

The study entailed the construction of a detail computer simulation developed from the construction drawings of the building, for the entire building, and was subjected to vigorous testing and verification. On page 111 of the report, Professor Hulsey concludes that:

> "The simultaneous failure of all core columns over 8 storeys followed 1.3 seconds later by the simultaneous failure of all exterior columns over 8 storeys produces almost exactly the behavior observed in videos of the collapse …
>
> It is our conclusion that the collapse of WTC 7 was a global failure involving the near simultaneous failure of all columns in the building and not a progressive collapse involving the sequential failure of columns throughout the building."

The US$300,000 four-year study was commissioned by Architects and Engineers for 911 Truth (AE911Truth), a section 501(c)(3) non-profit organisation which has 3,131 architects and engineers who have called for a new investigation into the collapse of all three buildings on 911, the Twin Towers of the World Trade Center (WTC1 & 2) and the 47-story WTC building number 7. WTC7, which was not hit by an airplane, collapsed straight down into its own footprint eight hours after the collapse of the Twin Towers just like a Controlled Demolition.

The report directly contradicts the report on the collapse of WTC7 by the National Institute of Standards and Technology (NIST) which was the official US Government agency tasked with explaining why the building fell down. NIST acknowledges that their explanation that office fires alone caused the collapse would have been the first time in history that a steel-framed high-rise building collapsed solely due to fire. NIST proposed the progressive collapse hypothesis as the basis of its conclusions which Hulsey's study now specifically disproves.

AE911Truth has expressed the view that the only way that they are aware of that such a collapse can occur is by the use of demolition charges. According to AE911Truth, no other plausible explanation is possible.

Since it takes months to prepare a building for demolition, for WTC7 to have collapsed just hours after the initial aircraft impacts, then the collapse must have been planned and prepared long before 911 occurred, by people who had unfettered access to the building in the weeks and months prior to 911. In other words,

**Professor Hulsey's report PROVES that 911 was an INSIDE JOB.**

This is NOT a 'crazy conspiracy theory'. This is now

PROVEN SCIENTIFIC FACT.

This material is communicated by David Frank Palmer on behalf of Truth Outreach Inc. AKA 911 Truth Action Project. This disclosure is made under the Foreign Influence Transparency Scheme Act 2018.

#3 This is the flyer whose title was subsequently changed to: *Scientific Report proves that 911 was an Inside Job* and from which the 911TAP logo and FITS declaration were removed.

# Flyer re US Court Cases

## U.S. Attorney in New York to Convene a Grand Jury to Consider Evidence that the World Trade Center Buildings Were Destroyed by Explosives

Petitions filed on April 10, 2018, 30th July 2018 and 12th March 2019 by the **Lawyers' Committee for 9/11 Inquiry** to the U.S. Attorney for the Southern District of New York present evidence that has been assembled by Architects and Engineers for 9/11 Truth in the last several years showing that explosives were used to take down three (yes, three!) buildings in New York City on 9/11/2001 and requesting that a grand jury be convened to consider this evidence.
The petitions with their 57 exhibits and supplementary information can be read at:
https://www.lawyerscommitteefor9-11inquiry.org/ via the "Grand Jury Petition" link at the top of the page.

A response dated November 7, 2018 sent from U.S. Attorney Geoffrey Berman's office stated that it will comply with the request for a grand jury investigation but it has refused to confirm that it has actually done so. On 6th September 2019 the Lawyers Committee applied to the court for a Writ of Mandamus to order the US Attorney to confirm he has done so or, if not, to now do so.

Legal procedures can be protracted so it could take some time, perhaps years, before the outcome of these initiatives is known but it is important to ensure that they are progressing. Grand juries are held in secret so they will not be open to the public but they are very powerful procedures that have the authority to summons and subpoena anyone they choose. The Lawyers' Committee for 9/11 Inquiry, which is a sister organization with the 9/11 Truth Action Project, is making every effort they can to assist in the grand jury process and to make sure it happens.

**For more information or to get involved and show your support, you can visit:**
**www.911tap.org, www.lcfor911.org, or**
**www.ae911truth.org.**

# Lawyers Committee for 911 Inquiry sues the US Department of Justice and the FBI

**Lawyers Committee for 911 Inquiry** filed suit in the District Court for the District of Columbia (case 1-19-cv-00824 filed 03/25/19 Document 1) against the United States Department of Justice and the Federal Bureau of Investigation for failing to comply with a 2014 federal law requiring the FBI, and 2014-15 911 Review Commission, to review and evaluate evidence available to it at the time of the Commission's inquiry and to report such evidence to congress. The suit requests the court to issue a Mandamus order for the defendants to now comply. The complaint cites seven classes of information the FBI and the 911 Review Commission failed to consider and report, including:

- the use of explosives to demolish WTC buildings 1,2 and 7;
- the arrest of five individuals, who self-identified as being Israeli, who later claimed that they were there to observe the event;
- video and photographic evidence collected by the FBI covering the Pentagon attack on that day;
- details of plane debris collected that day which contained serial numbers that could identify the planes they came from;
- apparent financial support to the alleged hijackers from Saudi sources including the Saudi royal family;

and

- anomalies in reports of calls from alleged passengers on hijacked airplanes to relatives on the ground on 911.

Details available here: https://www.911tap.org/557-news-releases/798-fbi-and-department-of-justice-sued-for-failure-to-perform-duties

# My advices to the Australian Federal Police

## Text of an e-mail sent by me to the Australian Federal Police on 14th September 2011

Hi Ross #4,

Further to our discussion over lunch at the Fremantle security conference at Friday, I am attaching the following as promised:

- A copy of my "911 Research Report – An Australian Perspective" which I e-mailed to my local MP, Mr Gary Grey, and to the national offices of the Liberal and Greens parties and to the state office of the Greens last November.

- A copy of the Addendum to my 911 Research Report that I sent to the same addressees after my return from Spain in May of this year

- A copy of the Harrit et al "Nanothermite" paper which is referred to in item 1 of my original report. This article is considered by the 911 Truth movement to be the "smoking gun" which proves that explosives were used to bring down the twin towers of the World Trade Centre (WTC) and WTC7. As my abovementioned reports show I have confirmed the authenticity of this report with its lead author, Professor Niels Harrit from the University of Copenhagen, and with Dr Frank Legge, an Australian co-author of the paper who lives in Perth.

- A copy of the English language version of a report by Professor Amparo Sacristan Carracso reporting the results of her analysis of the visual images of the aircraft that hit the South tower of the World Trade Centre on 911. In her report she concludes that the apparent anomalous cylindrical shapes attached to the underside of this aircraft are real physical objects. I believe that this report proves that the air aircraft that hit the South Tower of the World Trade Centre was not a commercial airliner. I have personally confirmed that conclusion with Professor Carrasco in a meeting with her in Barcelona, Spain in May of this year. I also have a copy of the attached report written in Spanish which Professor Carracso signed in my presence confirming the authenticity of her report and acknowledging that she still stands by its findings.

- I believe that both the Harrit et al "Nanothermite" paper and the Carrasco image analysis report constitute scientifically-based forensic evidence supporting the argument that the official United States Government explanation on what happened on 911 is wrong. The rest of my 911 report cites the secondary source evidence that I have also relied upon to arrive at my two substantive conclusions, namely:

a) That the official United States Government's narrative on 911 is not believable, and

b) That the "Controlled Demolition" hypothesis as to why World Trade Centre buildings WTC1, WTC2 and WTC7 collapsed is a more plausible explanation than the official "Pancake Collapse" hypothesis promoted in the US Government's version. Since a controlled demolition would require months of preparation it follows that if the "Controlled Demolition" hypothesis is proved to be correct one must also conclude that:

i.    911 was not a surprise attack, and

ii.   There must have been inside help to carry out these attacks. Since WTC7 contained the New York office of the CIA and also offices of the Defense Department, the Securities and Exchange Commission and the New York emergency management office, it is reasonable to assume that access to this building, at least, would have been restricted to persons with appropriate security clearances.

Whilst this is a very sensitive diplomatic issue for Australia, it is nevertheless, I believe, an appropriate matter for the AFP to investigate given that 911 was undoubtedly a mass murder and that ten Australian citizens are known to have died either in New York city or in Washington DC on the 11th of September, 2001 as a result of this event.

I will be happy to elaborate further on this material should you require.

Thank you for your patience and attention last Friday.

Cheers.

David.


# 4 The officer I met and sent this e-mail to provided me with his business card which identified him as being:

F/A Ross Hinscliff

T/L Intelligence

Perth.

# Stop Press

The very latest relevant news from the Lawyers Committee for 911 Inquiry Inc. (in an e-mail dated 15th May 2021) with respect to the two lawsuits reported in this compendium reads, in part:

"We are presently responding to two negative federal court rulings. One ruling in Washington D.C. concerned the 9/11 Review Commission where the FBI failed to evaluate and report to Congress on seven areas of 9/11 evidence which was never assessed by the original 9/11 Commission. In this case our Appellate Court Appeal was denied. However, the Lawyers' Committee is preparing a petition of certiorari to the United States Supreme Court. In NYC, the Southern District, Manhattan, the United States Attorney has failed, to our knowledge, to present to a Grand Jury the controlled demolition evidence given to him by the Lawyers' Committee showing that explosions were used to destroy the World Trade Center Towers. The courts ruling denying plaintiffs claims is being appealed. In both cases the issue of standing has been used by the government and the courts to deny the Lawyers' Committee's efforts to secure the truth.

It is hard to believe that co-plaintiffs Bob Mcilvaine who lost his son, Diana Hetzel who lost her husband, a NYC fire fighter, Jeane Evans who lost her brother, a NYC fire fighter, and NYC Hazmat Fire Chief Michael J. O'Kelly who suffered permanent lung damage working on the contaminated piles along with Fire Commissioner Christopher Gioia, Richard Gage, Architects and Engineers and the Lawyers' Committee would not have standing either under Federal Mandamus Law or the First Amendment of the United States Constitution Right to Petition Government."

The above-mentioned petition of certiorari to the United States Supreme Court was filed on 16th July, 2021.

So, the quest continues.

# About the Author

DAVID FRANK PALMER is a retired seventy-two-year-old former management consultant who specialized in strategic business planning for twenty-five years.

To date, David has published one philosophical essay, entitled *A Thesis on the Nature of Religion,* on the Centre for Globalization Research website. He has written and self-published a non-fiction book on mature-age entrepreneurship, entitled *Creating your Self-Employed Third Age Career.* He also published a speculative fiction novel, entitled *Armaginning,* through Zeus Publications of Brisbane in 2009, which drew on his technical, strategic planning knowledge of forecasting methodologies, his travel experiences, his two business degrees and a Graduate Diploma in International Relations.

His second novel, *Amerissance, American Renaissance,* was published by Linellen Press in 2020.